序 言

　　「ECL 測驗」的字彙題，看起來簡單，但裡面常會有一些很難的單字出現，如：ECL 考試曾出現過的 augur（預言家）、echelon（指揮階層）、extemporaneously（即席地）、bureaucratic（官僚的）、lubrication（潤滑），及聽力測驗中的 poise（姿態），如果你老是背一些簡單的單字，你的分數就沒辦法突出。「**ECL 字彙**」網羅了所有 ECL 已經考過的字彙，及 ALC 中，所有的重要字彙，只要把這本單字讀完，考任何「ECL 測驗」，都難不倒你。

　　單字是學好英文的基礎，背單字是一項毅力的考驗，剛開始背的時候，也許背了會忘，可是你會愈背愈快，背單字能夠去除煩惱，你會愈背愈愉快。你只要拼命背單字一個月，奇蹟就會出現，英文實力將大幅提升。

　　編者曾經在「美國國防語言學院」（American Defense Language Institute），參加過「英語教官複訓班」，參加過無數次的 ECL 測驗，深知出題方向，最重要的就是，文法、單字，和成語。讀者參加考試以前，只要將這部份讀熟，再加上不斷地練習聽力測驗，ECL 就可以得到滿分。

　　本書雖經審慎編校，疏漏之處，恐在所難免，尚祈各界先進不吝指正。

編者　謹識

🚁 CONTENTS

A

abandon 〔 ə'bændən 〕
v. 放棄

The police ***abandoned*** the search for the missing hikers.

警方放棄搜索下落不明的徒步旅行者。

abbreviation
〔 ə,brivɪ'eʃən 〕 *n.* 縮寫

Apr. is an ***abbreviation*** for April.

Apr.是 April（四月）的縮寫。

ability 〔 ə'bɪlətɪ 〕
n. 能力

Lacking the ***ability*** to repair the car himself, he took it to a mechanic.

因為他缺乏自己修車的能力，所以就把車開去找技工。

abnormal 〔 æb'nɔrml̩ 〕
adj. 不正常的

The cold weather is ***abnormal*** for this time of year. 在一年的這時候，出現寒冷的天氣是不正常的。

ab	+ norm + al
away from +	rule + adj.

aboard 〔 ə'bord 〕 *adv.*
到（車、船、飛機）上

The plane departed as soon as all the passengers were ***aboard***.

所有的乘客一登機，飛機就起飛了。

abrupt 〔 ə'brʌpt 〕 *adj.*
突然的

The bus driver made an ***abrupt*** turn, causing the passengers to stumble.

公車司機突然轉彎，使得乘客跌倒。

absolute（'æbsə,lut）
adj. 絕對的

The dictator has *absolute* control over the country.
獨裁者對全國有絕對的控制權。

absolutely
（,æbsə'lutlɪ）*adv.* 完全地；非常

I am *absolutely* sure that I left my keys on the desk.
我非常確定我把鑰匙留在書桌上。

absorb（əb'sɔrb）*v.* 吸收

The dry earth has already *absorbed* the rain. 乾燥的土壤已經把雨水都吸收了。

abundance（ə'bʌndəns）*n.* 豐富

The *abundance* of rice means that the price will go down.
稻米的豐收意謂著價格將會下跌。

abundant（ə'bʌndənt）*adj.* 豐富的

The country has an *abundant* supply of oil. 這個國家有豐富的石油。

access（'æksɛs）*n.* 使用權

Your membership fee gives you *access* to all of the club's facilities.
你繳的會費使你有權使用俱樂部的所有設備。

accessory（æk'sɛsərɪ）*n.* 配件

The store sells computers and software as well as computer *accessories*.
這家店不但有賣電腦和軟體，而且還賣電腦配件。

accidental

(ˌæksəˈdɛntḷ) *adj.* 偶然
的；意外的

His presence at the meeting was
accidental. He had intended to go
to room 404, but came to room 604
instead.

他會出席這場會議純粹是意外。他本來打
算要到 404 室，但卻跑到 604 室來。

accompany

(əˈkʌmpənɪ) *v.* 陪伴

The manager asked me to ***accompany***
the sick worker to the hospital.

經理要我陪這名生病的員工到醫院去。

accomplish

(əˈkɑmplɪʃ) *v.* 完成；
達成

We must ***accomplish*** the task by the
end of the week.

我們必須在這星期結束前完成工作。

accumulate

(əˈkjumjəˌlet) *v.* 積聚；
累積

It snowed heavily and soon three
inches had ***accumulated*** on the ground.

雪下得很大，所以一下子就在地上積了三
吋高的雪。

```
ac  +  cumulate
|         |
to  +  heap up
```

accuracy (ˈækjərəsɪ)
n. 正確性；準確性

The typist is known for her great
accuracy.

這名打字員以非常準確而聞名。

```
ac  +   cur    + acy
|       |         |
to  + take care + adj.
```

accurate ('ækjərɪt) *adj.*
精確的

A surgeon must be very *accurate* when he performs an operation.
外科醫生在動手術時，必須非常精確。

achieve (ə'tʃiv) *v.* 達到

He eventually *achieved* his goal of becoming a doctor.
他終於達到成為一名醫生的目標。

acid ('æsɪd) *n.*
【化學】酸類

Our teacher warned us to be careful with the *acid* during the experiment lest we get burned.
老師警告我們，在做實驗時要小心酸類，以免被灼傷。

act (ækt) *v.* 表現；行為

If you do not *act* appropriately, you may not be invited again.
如果你表現不當，可能就不會再被邀請。

activate ('æktə,vet) *v.*
使活動；使起作用

You can *activate* the fan with a touch of the finger.
你可以用手指觸碰風扇，使它開始運轉。

active ('æktɪv) *adj.* 活潑
的；活躍的

Sally is an *active* girl who enjoys sports, so she does not have to worry about her weight.
莎莉是個喜歡運動的活潑女孩，所以她不必擔心自己的體重。

activity 〔 æk'tɪvətɪ 〕 *n.*
活動

Our club arranges many *activities* for us such as field trips and competitions.
我們社團替我們安排許多像是實地考察旅行和比賽之類的活動。

actor 〔'æktɚ 〕 *n.* 男演員

The *actor* began his career in movies at an early age.
這名男演員在很年輕的時候，就開始他的電影事業。

actress 〔'æktrɪs 〕 *n.*
女演員

The *actress* was delighted when she won an award for her part in the movie. 當這名女演員在這部電影中的角色得獎時，她非常高興。

actual 〔'æktʃuəl 〕 *adj.*
實際的

The repairman's estimate was 10,000 dollars, but the *actual* price was 12,000. 這名修理工人估的價錢是一萬元，但實際的價格是一萬二。

actuate 〔'æktʃu,et 〕 *v.*
啓動

The machine can be *actuated* by remote control.
這部機器可以用遙控來啓動。

adapt 〔 ə'dæpt 〕 *v.* 適應

The visitors from Canada found it hard to *adapt* to the hot weather.
從加拿大來的觀光客，覺得要適應這裡炎熱的天氣很困難。

adequate (ˈædəkwɪt)
adj. 足夠的

Do we have an *adequate* amount of food for the party?
我們有足夠的食物供應這場宴會嗎？

adhere (ədˈhɪr) *v.*
黏著；遵守 < *to* >

The poster fell off the wall because the type of glue you used will not *adhere* to wood.
那張海報從牆上掉下來，因為你用的那種膠水，沒辦法把它黏在木頭上。

```
ad + here
 |      |
to + stick
```

Although he agreed to the rules of the game, he did not *adhere* to them.
雖然他贊成這些比賽規則，但卻沒有遵守。

adjust (əˈdʒʌst) *v.* 調整

If you are too cold, I can *adjust* the temperature of the air conditioner.
如果你太冷，我可以調整冷氣機的溫度。

admiral (ˈædmərəl) *n.*
海軍上將；海軍將領

Admiral is the highest rank in the navy.
海軍上將是海軍裡最高的階級。

admire (ədˈmaɪr) *v.*
讚賞；欽佩

Our teacher asked us to write an essay on the political leader we *admire* most.
我們老師要求我們寫一篇作文，談論自己最欽佩的政治領袖。

admit 〔 əd'mɪt 〕 v. 准許
進入；承認

The manager refused to *admit* the man to the restaurant because he was not wearing shoes.

經理拒絕讓這個人進入餐廳，因爲他沒穿鞋子。

Joyce *admitted* cheating on the test and apologized.

喬依絲承認考試作弊，並且道歉。

adult 〔 ə'dʌlt 〕 n. 成人

This movie is for *adults* only; it is not suitable for children.

這部電影只限成人觀賞；它不適合小孩看。

advance 〔 əd'væns 〕
v. 晉升

Most junior high school students hope to *advance* to senior high school.

大多數的國中生都希望能升上高中。

advanced 〔 əd'vænst 〕
adj. 高深的；高級的

After completing the intermediate class, you may go on to the *advanced* class.　在完成了中級課程之後，你也許可以去上高級課程。

advantage
〔 əd'væntɪdʒ 〕 n. 優點

One of the *advantages* of living in the city is convenient public transportation.

住在城市的其中一個優點，就是有便利的大衆運輸工具。

adventures
〔 əd'vɛntʃəz 〕 *n. pl.*
冒險故事

My grandfather likes to tell stories about his *adventures* in the navy.
我祖父喜歡說關於他在海軍服役時的冒險故事。

advertise 〔'ædvə͵taɪz 〕
v. 登廣告

To attract new workers, the company plans to *advertise* job openings in the newspaper. 爲了要吸引新員工,這家公司打算在報紙上刊登有職缺的廣告。

advertisement
〔͵ædvə'taɪzmənt 〕 *n.* 廣告

According to the *advertisement* in the newspaper, the sale will last all week.
根據報紙上所登的廣告,這次的拍賣將會持續整個星期。

affect 〔 ə'fɛkt 〕 *v.* 影響

A typhoon will often *affect* the price of vegetables. 颱風常會影響蔬菜的價格。

afford 〔 ə'ford 〕 *v.*
負擔得起

I would like to buy a new car but I can't *afford* it, so I am looking for a used one. 我想買一輛新車,可是買不起,所以我正在找二手車。

Africa 〔'æfrɪkə 〕
n. 非洲

The tourists traveled the length of Africa, starting in Egypt and ending in South *Africa*.
這群觀光客從非洲的一端到另一端旅行,從埃及出發,最後到南非共和國。

afterwards
〔'æftəwədz 〕 *adv.* 之後

We plan to listen to the speeches first and serve dinner *afterwards*.
我們打算先聽演說，之後再供應晚餐。

aid 〔 ed 〕 *n. v.* 幫助

The boy came to the *aid* of the blind man and led him across the busy street.　那名男孩前來幫助這個盲人，牽著他橫越熱鬧的街道。

A good dictionary will *aid* you in your studies.
一本好的字典有助於你的學業。

aim 〔 em 〕 *n.* 目標
v. 用（槍）瞄準

Becoming a famous musician is his *aim* in life.　成爲一位有名的音樂家，是他的人生目標。

The soldier *aimed* his gun at the target and fired.
這名士兵用他的槍瞄準目標，然後開槍。

aircraft 〔'ɛr,kræft 〕
n. 飛機

The control tower assigned the *aircraft* to runway two.
塔台指定這架飛機到第二跑道。

airman 〔'ɛrmən 〕
n. 飛行員

The plane crashed, but the *airman* was able to eject safely.
這架飛機墜毀了，不過飛行員已平安地彈射出去。

airtight (ˈɛrˌtaɪt) *adj.* 密閉的

The food must be packed in an *airtight* container or it will spoil.

食物必須裝在密閉的容器裡，否則會腐壞。

aisle (aɪl) *n.* 走道

When I checked in for the flight I was asked if I wanted to sit by the window or on the *aisle*.

當我去辦理登機手續時，被詢問是要坐靠窗還是靠走道的位子。

alcohol (ˈælkəˌhɔl) *n.* 酒；酒精

This restaurant does not serve *alcohol*, but you can order a soft drink.

這家餐廳沒有供應酒，但是你可以點不含酒精的飲料。

algebra (ˈældʒəbrə) *n.* 代數

Tim was doing well in math until he began to study *algebra*. 提姆在開始學代數之前，數學的成績都很好。

alive (əˈlaɪv) *adj.* 活的

The house collapsed, but the occupants were found *alive* in the basement.

這棟房子倒塌了，不過在地下室發現，住戶們還活著。

allergic (əˈlɝdʒɪk) *adj.* 過敏的 < *to* >

Pam will get sick if she eats seafood because she is *allergic* to it.

潘如果吃海鮮，就會身體不舒服，因為她對海鮮過敏。

allowance (ə'lauəns)
n. 零用錢

Mike asked his parents to increase his *allowance* in return for doing more household chores.
麥克要求父母增加他的零用錢，並以多做一些家事作爲交換。

alloy (ə'lɔɪ) *n.* 合金

Pewter is an *alloy*; it is composed of more than one metal.
白鑷是一種合金；它是由一種以上的金屬所組成。

```
al + loy
 |    |
to + bind
```

alongside (ə'lɔŋ'saɪd)
adv. 在…旁邊 < *of* >

The child stood *alongside* of his mother. 這個小孩站在他母親身邊。

alternate ('ɔltənɪt)
v. 輪流

My brother and I *alternate* doing the dishes. He washes them on Monday, I do it on Tuesday, and so on.
我弟弟和我輪流洗碗。他洗星期一，我洗星期二…等等。

altimeter ('æltə,mitə)
n. 高度計

With the *altimeter* out of order, it was impossible for the pilot to know what his altitude was. 因爲高度計故障了，所以飛行員不可能知道他所處的高度。

altitude ('æltə,tjud)
n. 高度

The plane flew at an *altitude* of 30,000 feet.
這架飛機在三萬英呎的高度飛行。

```
alt + itude
 |     |
high +  n.
```

aluminum
(ə'lumɪnəm) *n.* 鋁

Aluminum is a light and flexible metal. 鋁是一種又輕又易彎曲的金屬。

amaze (ə'mez) *v.*
使吃驚

Your ability to paint so well *amazes* me. 你有能力畫得這麼好，使我大吃一驚。

ambulance
('æmbjələns) *n.* 救護車

The police called an *ambulance* to take the injured man to the hospital.
警方叫了一輛救護車，把傷者送到醫院去。

ammunition
(,æmjə'nɪʃən) *n.* 彈藥

The robber ran out of *ammunition* and then surrendered to the police.
搶匪在彈藥用盡之後，向警方投降了。

ample ('æmpḷ) *adj.*
充足的

There is an *ample* amount of ice for the party.
有足夠的冰塊供宴會使用。

```
am   + ple
 |      |
about + full
```

amplifier
('æmplə,faɪɚ) *n.* 擴音器

Because the stadium is so large, the band will use *amplifiers* during the concert.
因為這個體育場太大了，所以這個樂團在舉行演唱會時將使用擴音器。

amplify ('æmplə,faɪ)
v. 擴大

His voice was *amplified* by the PA system so that everyone on campus could hear him.
他利用大眾廣播系統將聲音擴大，使得在校園內的人都能聽見他的聲音。

amusement
(ə'mjuzmənt) *n.* 娛樂

His only *amusement* is going to a movie once a week.

他唯一的娛樂就是一星期去看一次電影。

anesthetic
(͵ænəs'θɛtɪk) *n.* 麻醉劑

The doctor gave the patient an *anesthetic* to dull the pain.

醫生給病人施打麻醉劑，以減輕痛苦。

angle ('æŋg!) *n.* 角；
角度

The sofa is set at a right *angle* to the wall.

這張沙發是放在和牆壁呈直角的位置。

anniversary
(͵ænə'vɜsərɪ) *n.*
週年紀念日

My parents celebrated their 25th wedding *anniversary* last week.

我爸媽上個星期慶祝他們的二十五週年結婚紀念日。

announce (ə'naʊns)
v. 宣佈

The results of the election will be *announced* at midnight.

選舉的結果將在午夜宣佈。

```
an + nounce
 |      |
 to + report
```

annoy (ə'nɔɪ) *v.* 使心煩

The noise of the construction *annoys* me. 施工的噪音使我心煩。

antenna (æn'tɛnə)
n. 天線

Without the *antenna*, we cannot receive a radio signal.

沒有天線，我們就收不到無線電廣播的信號了。

anthem (ˈænθəm) *n.*
頌歌；讚美的歌曲

In the Olympic Games, the national *anthem* of a winner will be played when he accepts his medal.
在奧運會中，得獎者在領獎時，大會會播放他的國歌。

antique (ænˈtik) *n.*
古董

The chair is an *antique*; I inherited it from my grandparents.
這張椅子是古董；我從我祖父母那裡繼承來的。

anyplace (ˈɛnɪˌples)
adv. 任何地方

Sit *anyplace* you like; the seats are not reserved.
你喜歡坐任何地方都可以；這些座位沒有被預訂。

anyway (ˈɛnɪˌwe)
adv. 無論如何；還是

Although you are just a beginner, you must try *anyway*.
雖然你只是個初學者，你還是必須試一試。

It was raining, but we went out *anyway*.
當時正在下雨，但我們還是出去了。

appear (əˈpɪr) *v.*
似乎

Your arm *appears* to be broken; we'll have to take an X-ray to be sure.
你的手臂似乎骨折了；我們必須拍張 X 光片來確認。

appearance
〔ə'pırəns〕*n.* 外表

The old man looks weak, but don't be fooled by his *appearance*; he is actually very strong.

那位老先生看起來很虛弱，但是不要被他的外表騙了；他其實是非常強壯的。

appetite〔'æpə,taɪt〕
n. 食慾

I always have a good *appetite* after exercise. 我運動過後，食慾一向很好。

application
〔,æplə'keʃən〕*n.* 申請書

He filled out an *application* for the job before his interview. 在他去面試之前，先填好了這份工作的申請書。

apply〔ə'plaɪ〕*v.* 施加

You should *apply* pressure to a cut to stop the bleeding.

你應該對傷口施壓以止血。

approach〔ə'protʃ〕
v. 接近

Don't try to run away when a growling dog *approaches* you.

當一隻咆哮的狗接近你時，不要試著逃跑。

```
ap + proach
 |      |
to  +  near
```

appropriate
〔ə'propriɪt〕*adj.* 適當的

Casual clothes are not *appropriate* dress for a formal party.

平常穿的衣服對正式的宴會而言，並不適合。

```
ap + propri + ate
 |      |      |
to + proper + adj.
```

approval 〔 ə'pruvḷ 〕
n. 批准;贊成

The commander gave his *approval* of our plan.
指揮官批准了我們的計劃。

approximate
〔 ə'prɑksəmɪt 〕 *adj.*
大約的

The suspect's *approximate* age is twenty. 這名嫌疑犯年約二十歲。

```
ap + proximate
 |       |
to  +  nearest
```

architect〔'ɑrkə,tɛkt 〕
n. 建築師

The *architect* has designed several modern buildings.
這名建築師設計了好
幾棟現代化的建築物。

```
archi +  tect
  |       |
chief + builder
```

argue〔'ɑrgju 〕*v.*
爭論;爭吵

My sister and I often *argue*, but we soon make up again.
我姊姊和我常吵架,但我們很快就又和好了。

argument
〔'ɑrgjəmənt 〕*n.* 爭論;
爭吵

The children had an *argument* over whose turn it was to play with the toy.
孩子們為了輪到誰玩玩具而爭吵。

arm〔 ɑrm 〕*v.* 使武裝;
使配備(武器)

The rebels are being *armed* by the opposition party.
這群反叛者是由反對黨提供武器的。

armor（'armɚ）*n.*
（軍艦、戰車等的）
裝甲；防護鋼板

The *armor* of the tank cannot be
pierced by bullets.
子彈無法貫穿這輛坦克車的防護鋼板。

around（ə'raʊnd）
prep. 環繞…周圍

She tied some string *around* the package
before mailing it.　在寄出包裹前，她用一
些繩子捆住包裹的周圍。

arrange（ə'rendʒ）
v. 排列；安排

The librarian *arranged* the books on the
shelves in alphabetical order.
這名圖書館員將那些書按照
字母序排列在架子上。

```
ar + range
 |     |
to + rank
```

We *arranged* to meet at the restaurant at
six o'clock.　我們約六點在這家餐廳見面。

arrow（'æro）*n.* 箭；
箭頭

This *arrow* tells us that it is a one-way
street.　這個箭頭告訴我們，這是一條單行道。

artery（'ɑrtərɪ）
n. 動脈

Too much fat in your diet may lead to
blocked *arteries*.
日常飲食中含有太多脂肪，可能會導致動
脈阻塞。

artificial
（,ɑrtə'fɪʃəl）
adj. 人造的

The flowers are not real; they are
artificial.
這些花不是真的；它們是人造的。

artillery 〔 ɑr'tɪlərɪ 〕
n. 大砲

The colonel was put in charge of the ***artillery***.

這名上校被派去管理大砲。

ascend 〔 ə'sɛnd 〕 v.
上升

After takeoff the plane will ***ascend*** to an altitude of 30,000 feet.

這架飛機在起飛之後,將會
上升到三萬英呎的高度。

a + scend
to + climb

ascent 〔 ə'sɛnt 〕 n.
攀登;上升

The ***ascent*** up the mountain was long and difficult, but the view was worth it.

攀登這座山要花很長的時間,而且又困難,
但是它的景色卻值得一看。

aspirin 〔 'æspərɪn 〕 n.
阿斯匹靈

The nurse gave me some ***aspirin*** for my headache.

這名護士給我一些阿斯匹靈,來治療我的
頭痛。

assemble 〔 ə'sɛmbl̩ 〕
v. 裝配

After taking the air conditioner apart, he was unable to ***assemble*** it again.

在把冷氣機拆開之後,他沒辦法再把它裝
回去。

assign 〔 ə'saɪn 〕 v.
分派;指派

The task of preparing the meeting hall was ***assigned*** to Bill.

準備會議廳的工作,被分派給比爾。

assignment
〔 ə'saɪnmənt 〕 *n.* 任務；
工作

His first *assignment* after basic
training was on an aircraft carrier.
他完成基本訓練後的第一份工作，是在一
架航空母艦上。

assist〔 ə'sɪst 〕 *v.* 幫助

My grandmother needs someone to
assist her when she climbs the stairs.
我祖母爬樓梯時，需要有
人幫忙。

as +	sist
to +	stand

associate〔 ə'soʃɪˌet 〕
v. 交往

The soldiers were warned not to
associate with the local people.
士兵們被警告，不能跟當地人來往。

assume〔 ə'sum 〕 *v.*
以為

When Dave did not come to class,
I *assumed* that he was ill.
當戴夫沒來上課時，我以為他生病了。

assure〔 ə'ʃur 〕 *v.*
保證

Having *assured* himself that the door
was locked, he left.
他確定門鎖上之後，就
離開了。

as +	sure
to +	sure

I *assure* you that your order will
arrive within three days.
我向你保證，你訂購的東西會在三天以內
送達。

atmosphere

('ætməs,fɪr) *n.* 大氣層

Exhaust from factories pollutes the earth's *atmosphere*.
工廠排出的廢氣，污染了地球的大氣層。

atmo	+	sphere
vapor	+	*ball*

atom ('ætəm) *n.* 原子

An *atom* is too small to be seen with the naked eye. 原子太小了，肉眼是看不見的。

a	+	tom
not	+	*divide* (不能再分割)

atomic (ə'tɑmɪk)
adj. 原子的

Atomic energy is an important resource for many countries.
原子能對許多國家而言，是重要的資源。

attach (ə'tætʃ) *v.*
黏貼；附上 < *to* >

Please *attach* your resume to your application form.
請將你的履歷表附在你的申請書上。

attempt (ə'tɛmpt)
v. 試著；企圖

We will *attempt* to finish the work by Friday.
我們會試著在星期五之前，完成這份工作。

at	+	tempt
to	+	*try*

attend (ə'tɛnd) *v.*
上 (學) ；參加

You must *attend* the class every day, or you will not be able to pass.
你必須天天去上課，否則你考試可能會不及格。

attendance
〔 ə'tɛndəns 〕 *n.* 出席；
出席人數

Your *attendance* is requested at the meeting. 敬請出席這場會議。

The *attendance* at the speech was small. 這場演講的出席人數很少。

attention 〔 ə'tɛnʃən 〕
n. 注意力

Paying *attention* to what others say will help you to communicate better.
注意別人說的話，將有助於使你和別人溝通。

attitude 〔 'ætə,tjud 〕
n. 態度；姿勢

Sam is always happy because he has a positive *attitude*.
因為山姆的態度樂觀，所以他一向很快樂。

【比較】 <u>at</u>titude（態度）
<u>al</u>titude（高度）
凡是字尾是 tude，重音在倒數第三個音節上。

attract 〔 ə'trækt 〕 *v.*
吸引

The bright flowers *attract* many bees.
色彩鮮艷的花朵吸引了許多蜜蜂。

at + tract
　|　　|
to + draw

attractive 〔 ə'træktɪv 〕
adj. 吸引人的

The girl looked very *attractive* in her new dress.
那個女孩穿著她的新洋裝，看起來非常吸引人。

author (ˈɔθɚ) *n.* 作者；作家

Although still young, the *author* has already published three books.

這名作家雖然還很年輕，卻已經出版了三本書。

authority (əˈθɔrətɪ) *n.* 權力；權威

I'm sorry. I don't have the *authority* to give you a refund, but I will ask the manager.

很抱歉，我沒有權力退錢給你，但是我會去問經理。

auxiliary (ɔgˈzɪljərɪ) *adj.* 輔助的

The city has an *auxiliary* police force, which helps out during special events.

這個城市擁有在發生特殊事件時，會出面協助的輔助警力。

available (əˈveləbḷ) *adj.* 可獲得的

There is an apartment *available* in the building.

在這棟建築物內，可以買到一間公寓。

average (ˈævərɪdʒ) *adj.* 平均的

The *average* temperature in summer is thirty-five degrees.

夏天的平均溫度是三十五度。

aviation (ˌevɪˈeʃən) *n.* 航空學

Paul studies *aviation* because he wants to be a pilot one day.

保羅研讀航空學，因爲他以後想當飛行員。

avoid 〔 ə'vɔɪd 〕
v. 避免

My brother will do almost anything to *avoid* having to do the dishes because he hates housework.
我哥哥會想盡辦法逃避洗碗的工作，因爲他討厭做家事。

aware 〔 ə'wɛr 〕 *adj.*
知道的

I got a ticket because I was not *aware* of the traffic laws.
因爲我不懂交通規則，所以被開了一張罰單。

awfully 〔'ɔflɪ 〕 *adv.*
非常地

Ted was *awfully* sick after he ate some bad seafood.
泰德吃了一些劣質海鮮後，病得很重。

axis 〔'æksɪs 〕 *n.* 軸

The earth rotates on its *axis* once every 24 hours.
地球每二十四小時繞著地軸自轉一周。

【劉毅老師的話】

　　背單字可以訓練自己的記憶，解除煩惱，考驗自己的毅力。

B

backbone 〔'bæk'bon 〕
n. 脊椎骨

The *backbone* is made up of many vertebrae.
脊椎是由許多脊椎骨所組成的。

background
〔'bæk͵graʊnd 〕*n.* 背景

The situation is impossible to understand unless you know the *background*.
除非你知道這件事發生的背景，否則不可能了解情況。

balance 〔'bæləns 〕
n. 餘額

We paid 75% of the damage and the other driver paid the *balance* of the repair bill.
我們付了百分之七十五的損壞修理費用，而另一個駕駛人則付剩下的部分。

bald 〔 bɔld 〕*adj.* 禿頭的

The man began to lose his hair at a young age and was completely *bald* by the time he reached thirty.
這名男子從年輕時就開始掉頭髮，當他三十歲時，已經幾乎禿頭了。

ballet 〔 bæ'le 〕*n.*
芭蕾舞劇

The gracefulness of the dancers in the *ballet* was amazing.
芭蕾舞劇中，舞者的優雅舞姿令人驚嘆。

bandage〔'bændɪdʒ〕
n. 繃帶

The nurse applied a ***bandage*** to the injury.
護士在傷口上貼上繃帶。

bar〔bɑr〕*n.*（木、金屬等的）條

The windows of the jewelry store were protected by metal ***bars***.
珠寶店的窗戶用金屬柵欄做防護。

barbecue〔'bɑrbɪ,kju〕
n. 烤肉架

We cooked the steaks on a ***barbecue*** when we had our picnic.
野餐時，我們在烤肉架上烹煮牛排。

bare〔bɛr〕*adj.* 赤裸的

The boy got a terrible sunburn on his ***bare*** back.
這男孩赤裸的背被曬得很黑。

barely〔'bɛrlɪ〕*adv.*
幾乎不

I ***barely*** recognized my classmate because he lost a lot of weight over the summer.
我幾乎認不出我同學，因為他這個夏天瘦了很多。

barn〔bɑrn〕*n.* 穀倉

The farmer kept his cows in the ***barn*** during the storm.
在暴風雨期間，農夫將母牛關在穀倉裡。

barometer

〔 bəˈramətɚ 〕 *n.* 氣壓計

We can find out what the atmospheric pressure is by looking at a ***barometer***.

我們可以觀察氣壓器的數值，得知氣壓有多高。

```
baro  +  meter
  |        |
weight + measure (測定空氣的重量)
```

barrel 〔ˈbærəl 〕 *n.* 槍管

The soldier pointed the ***barrel*** of the gun at the target.

士兵們將槍管瞄準目標。

basic 〔ˈbesɪk 〕 *adj.* 基本的

The student has ***basic*** knowledge of the history of China and would like to learn more.

學生們對中國的歷史都有基本的認識，而且想要再多學一點。

basis 〔ˈbesɪs 〕 *n.* 根據；基礎

The cost of living was the ***basis*** of the workers' demand for higher pay.

工人們是根據生活上的花費來要求加薪。

battery 〔ˈbætərɪ 〕 *n.* 電池

We called a tow truck when we realized the car ***battery*** was dead.

當我們知道汽車的電池沒電時，就打電話叫拖車來。

beacon〔'bikən 〕*n.*
指標

The lighthouse was a *beacon* that warned
ships away from the dangerous rocks.
燈塔是一種指標，警告漁船遠離危險的礁石。

beam〔 bim 〕*n.* 光束

A flashlight cast a strong *beam* of light
down the dark stairway.
手電筒投射出強烈的光束，照著黑暗的樓梯。

bear〔 bɛr 〕*v.* 忍受

Some people find it difficult to *bear*
the heat of summer.
有些人覺得，夏天的酷熱令人難以忍受。

beard〔 bɪrd 〕*n.* 鬍子

Santa Claus is always pictured with a
long, white *beard*.
聖誕老人通常都被想像成，留有長長的白
鬍子。

bearings〔'bɛrɪŋz 〕
n. pl. 方向；方位

The compass helped us to keep our
bearings in the mountains.
指南針能幫助我們，在山裡不會迷失方向。

beauty〔'bjutɪ 〕*n.* 美

The *beauty* of the garden in spring is
beyond compare.
在春天時，這座花園的美是無與倫比的。

beer〔 bɪr 〕*n.* 啤酒

In the evening my father likes to drink
a glass of *beer*.
我爸爸喜歡在晚上喝杯啤酒。

behave〔 bɪˋhev 〕*v.*
表現

If you *behave* poorly at the party, I will not bring you again.
如果你在宴會上表現欠佳，我將不再帶你來參加。

behavior〔 bɪˋhevjɚ 〕
n. 行為

Opening doors for people is polite *behavior*.
幫別人開門是禮貌的行為。

bend〔 bɛnd 〕*v.* 使彎曲

A blacksmith can *bend* a piece of metal into the shape he wants.
鐵匠可以把一塊金屬彎成他想要的形狀。

beneath〔 bɪˋniθ 〕
prep. 在～之下

Please place your books on the shelf *beneath* your desk.
請將你的書放在書桌下的架子上。

beneficial
〔͵bɛnəˋfɪʃəl 〕*adj.* 有利的

The agreement was *beneficial* to everyone and was unanimously approved. 這個協議對每個人都有利，所以獲得全體一致的贊同。

```
bene + fic + ial
 |      |     |
well  + do  + adj.
```

beside〔 bɪˋsaɪd 〕*prep.*
在～旁邊

The waiter set the spoon *beside* the bowl. 服務生把湯匙放在碗旁邊。

besides ﹝ bɪ'saɪdz ﹞
adv. 此外

He cleaned not only the house, but the garage *besides*.
他不只打掃房子，還打掃車庫。

beyond ﹝ bɪ'jɑnd ﹞
prep. 在⋯的那一邊

You will find the library just *beyond* the park.
在公園的那一邊，你可以找到圖書館。

birth ﹝ bɝθ ﹞ *n.* 出生

The father was present at his son's *birth*.
這位父親在他兒子出生時是在場的。

birthday ﹝'bɝθ͵de﹞
n. 生日

We will celebrate my uncle's *birthday* with a cake.
我們會用蛋糕來幫叔叔慶祝生日。

bit ﹝ bɪt ﹞ *n.* 一點點

I'd like a *bit* of ice cream with my cake. 我想在蛋糕上加點冰淇淋。

bite ﹝ baɪt ﹞ *v.* 咬

It is said that barking dogs seldom *bite*. 聽說會叫的狗不會咬人。

blank ﹝ blæŋk ﹞ *n.*
空白

I wrote my name and address carefully in the *blanks* on the application form.
我在申請表的空格中，仔細填上姓名和地址。

blast〔blæst〕*n.* 爆炸；
強風

When the bomb went off, the *blast* was felt across the street.

當炸彈爆炸時，在對街都可以感受到一陣爆破的威力。

bleed〔blid〕*v.* 流血

My finger began to *bleed* after I cut it with the knife.

在我被刀子割傷手指後，它就開始流血。

blind〔blaɪnd〕*adj.* 盲的

A seeing eye dog is trained to help the *blind*.

導盲犬被訓練來幫助盲人。

blip〔blɪp〕*n.* 雷達上顯示的映像光點

The *blip* on the radar screen represented an airplane.

雷達螢幕上的光點，代表一架飛機。

blood〔blʌd〕*n.* 血

When I asked him why he had *blood* on his knee, he told me that he had fallen down the stairs.

當我問他膝蓋上為什麼會有血時，他告訴我他從樓梯上摔下來。

bloom〔blum〕*n.* 開花（的狀態或時期）

Our rose bush is in *bloom* now and is beautiful to see.

我們的玫瑰叢現在正在開花，看起來很美。

blossom (ˈblɑsəm)
n. 花

Viewing the cherry *blossoms* is a popular activity in spring.
賞櫻花是春天很受歡迎的活動。

blowout (ˈbloˌaut)
n. 爆胎

While driving on the highway, we had a *blowout* and had to change the tire.
當我們在公路上開車時，車子爆胎了，我們必須更換輪胎。

blunt (blʌnt) *adj.* 鈍的

It is not easy to cut fruit with a *blunt* knife.
用鈍掉的刀子切水果並不容易。

blurry (ˈblɝɪ) *adj.*
模糊不清的

Unfortunately the photograph is out of focus and *blurry*.
可惜的是，這張照片焦點沒對準，模糊不清。

board (bord) *v.*
上（車、船、飛機）

We are usually asked to *board* an airplane 20 minutes before takeoff.
我們通常會在飛機起飛前二十分鐘，被要求要登機。

board (bord) *n.* 木板

The carpenter joined the *boards* together and soon had constructed a cabinet. 木匠將木板接合，很快地就做出一個櫥櫃。

bolt 〔 bolt 〕 *n.* 門閂

For your safety, remember to put the *bolt* on the door at night.
爲了你的安全，晚上記得要把門閂栓上。

bomb 〔 bɑm 〕 *n.* 炸彈

The hijackers claimed to have smuggled a *bomb* onto the aircraft.
劫機者宣稱，他們已經將炸彈偷偷運上飛機。

booth 〔 buθ 〕 *n.* 攤亭

The man in the ticket *booth* says that the show is sold out. 在售票亭內的男子說，這場表演的票已經賣光了。

bore 〔 bor 〕 *v.* 鑽孔

The immigrants *bored* small holes in the box to breathe through.
這些移民在箱子上鑽了小孔，以便呼吸。

bounce 〔 baʊns 〕 *v.*
反彈

The basketball *bounced* off the backboard. 籃球從籃板上反彈回來。

bow 〔 baʊ 〕 *n.* 船首

The passengers liked to stand at the *bow* of the ship so that they could see where they were going.
乘客們都喜歡站在船首，這樣一來他們就可以看見行進的方向。

brain 〔 bren 〕 *n.* 大腦

The boy suffered *brain* damage after receiving a blow to the head.
那男孩在頭部遭到重擊後，腦部受損。

branch 〔 bræntʃ 〕 *n.*
部門

The legislature is the *branch* of government that makes laws.
立法院是政府負責制定法律的部門。

brand 〔 brænd 〕 *n.* 牌子

Nike is a famous *brand*.
耐吉是名牌。

brass 〔 bræs 〕 *n.* 黃銅

The shiny plates were made of *brass*.
這些閃閃發光的牌子是黃銅製的。

brave 〔 brev 〕 *adj.*
勇敢的

He was not *brave* enough to try riding the bicycle by himself.
他不夠勇敢，不敢嘗試自己一個人騎腳踏車。

breakdown
〔'brek,daʊn 〕 *n.* 故障；
崩潰

The misunderstanding happened due to a *breakdown* in communication.
這個誤會之所以發生，是由於溝通不良。

breathe 〔 brið 〕 *v.*
呼吸

It is impossible for mammals to *breathe* underwater.
哺乳類動物不可能在水中呼吸。

bridge 〔 brɪdʒ 〕 *n.* 橋

Before the *bridge* was built, the only way to cross the river was by boat.
這座橋尚未建造前，越過這條河唯一的辦法是搭船。

brief 〔 brif 〕 *v.* 對…作簡單說明

The president will *brief* the press on the situation at 3:00.

總統會在三點鐘，對新聞界簡單說明這個情況。

briefing 〔 'brifɪŋ 〕 *n.* 簡報

The manager gave his staff a *briefing* so that everyone could understand the problem.

經理對他的職員做了一個簡報，使每個人都能了解這個問題。

broke 〔 brok 〕 *adj.* 身無分文的

Although he makes a good salary, Jim is always *broke* by the end of the month.

儘管吉姆的薪水很高，但他卻總在月底時身無分文。

bronze 〔 brɑnz 〕 *adj.* 青銅製的　*n.* 青銅

There are many *bronze* artifacts at the museum.

博物館中有許多青銅製的手工藝品。

Bronze is a common alloy of two metals.

青銅是由兩種金屬組成的常用合金。

broom 〔 brum 〕 *n.* 掃帚

The housekeeper swept the floor with a *broom*.

女管家用掃帚掃地板。

brunette〔bruˈnɛt〕*n.*
頭髮及眼睛是褐色的女孩
【美國女孩通常分為 brunnette
和 blonde 兩種】

Some *brunettes* like to dye their hair blonde.
有些擁有深褐色頭髮的女孩，喜歡把她們的頭髮染成金色的。

bubble〔ˈbʌbḷ〕*n.*
泡沫

He used a lot of soap to wash the dishes and the sink filled with *bubbles*.
他用許多肥皂洗盤子，已致於整個水槽充滿泡沫。

bull〔bʊl〕*n.* 公牛

Fighting *bulls* is a popular sport in Spain. 鬥牛在西班牙是很受歡迎的運動。

bullet〔ˈbʊlɪt〕*n.* 子彈

He fired the gun, but the *bullet* missed its target.
他開了槍，可是子彈卻沒有命中目標。

bumpy〔ˈbʌmpɪ〕*adj.*
崎嶇不平的

The car bounced up and down on the *bumpy* road.
車子在崎嶇不平的道路上下顛簸。

bundle〔ˈbʌndḷ〕*n.* 捆

The boy picked up the *bundle* of newspapers and began to deliver them.
男孩將一捆報紙提起，並開始發送。

burst〔bɝst〕*v.* 爆破；
爆炸

The balloon *burst* with a loud bang.
氣球爆炸時發出一聲巨響。

C

cabin 〔'kæbɪn 〕*n.*
小木屋

In addition to their house in the city, they have a small *cabin* on the lake.

他們除了在城裡有一棟房子之外，還擁有一棟湖邊小木屋。

cable 〔'kebḷ 〕*n.* 電纜

The elevator is supported by strong steel *cables*.

電梯是由堅固的鋼鐵電纜所支撐。

cadet 〔kə'dɛt 〕*n.*
（陸海空）軍校學生

Cadets are required to wear their uniforms while at the military school.

軍校的學生在軍校內，必須穿著制服。

café 〔kə'fe 〕*n.* 咖啡廳

Let's meet at the *café* for a drink.

我們在咖啡廳碰面，喝杯飲料吧。

calculate 〔'kælkjə‚let 〕
v. 計算

The storekeeper *calculated* the total and then gave me my bill.

店主算出總額後，把帳單交給我。

calf 〔kæf 〕*n.* 小牛

The *calf* is too young to live without the mother cow.

小牛年紀太小，如果沒有母牛，就活不下去了。

calibrate (ˈkæləˌbret)
v. 校正；調整

We *calibrated* the thermometer by comparing it to the one in the science lab. 我們將這支溫度計和科學實驗室裡的那支比較，以調整刻度。

calm (kɑm) adj.
平靜的；無風浪的

On a windless day the lake is perfectly *calm*.
在無風的日子裡，湖面十分平靜。

camouflage
(ˈkæməˌflɑʒ) v. 掩飾；
隱藏

Soldiers wear clothes that blend in with the surroundings in order to *camouflage* themselves.
士兵們會為了隱藏自己，而穿著能與周遭環境融合的服裝。

cancel (ˈkænsḷ) v. 取消

We had to *cancel* our hotel reservation when we found we couldn't take the vacation after all.
當我們發現根本無法休假時，就把預訂的旅館取消了。

candle (ˈkændḷ) n. 蠟燭

It is customary to place *candles* on a birthday cake.
生日蛋糕上，都習慣插上蠟燭。

capability
(ˌkepəˈbɪlətɪ) n. 能力

Are you sure he has the *capability* to take charge of this project?
你確定他有能力負責這個計劃嗎？

capable (ˈkepəbḷ)
adj. 有能力的

She is not *capable* of lifting that heavy box by herself. 她沒有能力自己一個人把那個沉重的箱子搬起來。

capacity (kəˈpæsətɪ)
n. 容量

The *capacity* of the auditorium is 300 people. 這座大禮堂可容納三百人。

captain (ˈkæptɪn) *n.*
船長；上尉

The ship and its *captain* were welcomed in the port.
這艘船和它的船長在港口受到歡迎。

He had served as a *captain* for several years before he was promoted to the rank of major. 在他的官階升爲少校之前，他已經當了好幾年的上尉。

capture (ˈkæptʃɚ) *v.*
捕捉

The prisoners were *captured* while trying to escape.
這些囚犯在試圖逃脫時，被逮捕了。

carbon (ˈkɑrbən) *n.*
碳

Scientists are able to determine how old an object is through the process of *carbon* dating.
科學家們可以經由碳-14年代測定法的程序，確定某個物體已存在多久。

cargo (ˈkɑrgo) *n.*
貨物

The *cargo* was damaged because the delivery truck was in an accident.
因爲運送的卡車發生意外，所以貨物遭到毀損。

carpenter (ˈkɑrpəntɚ)
n. 木匠

That beautiful chair was handmade by a *carpenter*.
這把美麗的椅子，是木匠用手工製成的。

cartoon (kɑrˈtun) *n.*
卡通；漫畫

Political *cartoons* in the newspaper express people's concerns in a humorous way.
報紙上的政治漫畫是以幽默的方式，來表達人們對政治的關心。

cartridge (ˈkɑrtrɪdʒ)
n. 彈殼；墨水匣

After the robbery, the police found several *cartridges* in the bank, indicating that many shots had been fired.　在搶案發生後，警察在銀行裡發現了好幾個彈殼，顯示曾有許多子彈被發射。

case (kes) *n.* 情況

In this *case*, I believe we should put off our decision until tomorrow.
在這種情況下，我認爲我們應該延到明天再做決定。

catalog (ˈkætḷˌɔg) *n.*
目錄；大學概況手冊
（含校規、課程等）
（ = *catalogue* ）

The students studied the school *catalog*, eager to choose their new courses. 學生們研讀著學校的概況手冊，急著要選擇他們的新課程。

```
cata  +  log
 |        |
fully + speak （描述得很仔細）
```

category (ˈkætəˌgorɪ)
n. 種類;類別

My sister competed in the watercolor *category* at the art competition.
我姊姊參加美術比賽中的水彩畫組。

catsup (ˈkætsəp) *n.*
蕃茄醬
(**ketchup** (ˈkɛtʃəp))

What do you like on your hamburger, *catsup* or mustard?
你的漢堡要加什麼,蕃茄醬還是芥末?

cattle (ˈkætl̩) *n.*
牛 (集合名詞)

With so many *cattle* ranches in Australia, it is natural that people there eat a lot of beef.
在澳洲有非常多的大型牧牛場,所以當地人很自然地會吃很多牛肉。

cavity (ˈkævətɪ) *n.*
蛀洞

Finding a *cavity* in my tooth, the dentist said it had to be filled right away.
當牙醫發現我的牙齒蛀了一個洞時,他說必需馬上填補那顆牙齒。

```
cav  + ity
 |      |
hollow + n.
```

celebrate (ˈsɛləˌbret)
v. 慶祝

We *celebrated* our victory with a party at the coach's house.
我們在教練的家裡舉辦派對,來慶祝勝利。

cement (səˈmɛnt) *n.*
水泥

The drab *cement* walls of the school were painted a bright color.
學校淡褐色的水泥牆,被漆上了明亮的色彩。

central (ˈsɛntrəl)
adj. 中央的

Our new apartment is conveniently located because it is *central* to the downtown area.

我們的新公寓位於很便利的地點，因為它就在市中心的中央區域。

century (ˈsɛntʃərɪ)
n. 世紀

In the year 2000, we began not only a new *century*, but also a new millennium.

在兩千年這一年，不但是一個新世紀的開始，也是另一個新的一千年。

ceremony (ˈsɛrəˌmonɪ)
n. 典禮；儀式

A wedding *ceremony* is a happy occasion.

結婚典禮是一個快樂的場合。

certificate (səˈtɪfəkɪt)
n. 證書

The senior citizen was required to present his birth *certificate* to prove how old he was.

這位老人被要求出示出生證明，來證明自己的年紀。

challenge (ˈtʃælɪndʒ)
v. 挑戰

After losing the game, we immediately *challenged* the other team to a rematch.

在輸了這場比賽後，我們立刻向另一隊挑戰，要再比一次。

chamber (ˈtʃembɚ)
n. 槍膛

The officer removed the cartridge from the *chamber* and began to clean the weapon.

這位軍官將彈匣從槍膛中取出後，開始清理這件武器。

chapter (ˈtʃæptɚ) *n.*
章節

Our teacher assigned us three *chapters* in our history book to read over the weekend.

我們老師指定了歷史課本中的三個章節，要我們在週末閱讀。

character (ˈkærɪktɚ)
n. 性格

With such an optimistic *character*, he is rarely saddened by failure.

他生性樂觀，很少會因為失敗而悲傷。

characteristic
(ˌkærɪktəˈrɪstɪk) *n.* 特性

Generosity is one of the *characteristics* of his personality.

慷慨是他人格中的一個特性。

charge (tʃɑrdʒ) *v.*
充電

I asked the mechanic to *charge* the dead battery.

電池沒電了，我要求技工替我充電。

chart (tʃɑrt) *n.* 圖表

This *chart* shows that our sales figures have declined in the last six months.

這個圖表顯示，在過去六個月，我們的銷售數字已經減少了。

chemical (ˈkɛmɪkl̩)
n. 化學藥品

We were not allowed to use dangerous *chemicals* in our chemistry class.
我們不能在化學課上使用危險的化學藥品。

choke (tʃok) *v.*
使窒息；噎住

The diner *choked* on a fish bone and was unable to breathe.
這位用餐者被魚刺噎到，而無法呼吸。

chopper (ˈtʃɑpɚ) *n.*
直升機 (= *helicopter*)

A *chopper* hovered over the camp.
有架直升機在營地上方盤旋。

circuit (ˈsɚkɪt) *n.*
繞行一週

When my father goes jogging, he completes a *circuit* around the park three times.
我爸爸去慢跑時，他會繞著公園跑完三圈。

```
circu + it
  |     |
round + go
```

civil (ˈsɪvl̩) *adj.* 公民的

The protesters claimed that their *civil* rights had been violated.
抗議者宣稱，他們的公民權已受到侵犯。

claim (klem) *v.* 要求；
認領

The young man presented the winning ticket and *claimed* the reward.
這個年輕人出示中獎的彩券，並要求領取獎金。

classical (ˈklæsɪkḷ)
adj. 古典的

My aunt enjoys listening to *classical* music when she relaxes.
我阿姨喜歡在放鬆的時候，聽古典音樂。

classified
(ˈklæsəˌfaɪd) *adj.* 分類的

In the hope of finding a job, I read through the *classified* ads in the newspaper.
我從頭到尾看完了報紙上的分類廣告，希望能找到一份工作。

classify (ˈklæsəˌfaɪ)
v. 分類

We can *classify* this artifact as belonging to the Bronze Age.
我們可以將這件手工藝品，歸類爲是屬於青銅時代的產物。

clearance (ˈklɪrəns)
n. (可供車船通過的) 間隔距離；間隙

The sign says the *clearance* is only thirteen feet, so our truck is too big to go under this bridge.
這告示牌說，間隔只有十三呎，所以我們的卡車太大了，無法從橋下通過。

clever (ˈklɛvɚ) *adj.*
聰明的

Unfortunately, I am not *clever* enough to solve the problem. 可惜的是，我不夠聰明，無法解決這個問題。

client (ˈklaɪənt) *n.*
客戶；訴訟委託人

A successful attorney has many *clients*.
一個成功的律師，會擁有許多委託人。

cliff 〔 klɪf 〕 *n.* 懸崖

The driver fell asleep at the wheel of the car and drove off the *cliff*, landing on the rocks below.

那名駕駛人在開車時睡著了，而把車開下懸崖，掉到底下的岩石上。

clinic 〔'klɪnɪk 〕 *n.* 診所

Some people prefer to go to a *clinic* rather than a hospital when they are ill because they do not have to wait so long.

有些人生病時比較喜歡到診所去看病，而不去醫院，因為他們不用等很久。

clockwise 〔'klɑk,waɪz 〕 *adj.* 順時針方向的

The demonstrators walked around the building in a *clockwise* direction.

示威的人以順時針方向，繞著那棟建築物行走。

close 〔 klos 〕 *adj.* 靠近的

We are able to buy tickets for seats *close* to the stage.

我們可以買到靠近舞台的座位的票。

closed 〔 klozd 〕 *adj.* 關閉的

I'm sorry, but the office is *closed* now. You'll have to come back tomorrow.

很抱歉，但是辦公室現在已經關閉了。你必須明天再來。

club 〔klʌb〕 *n.* 俱樂部

We are going to the Officers' *Club* for dinner tonight.

我們今天晚上要到軍官俱樂部去用餐。

coarse 〔kors〕 *adj.* 粗糙的

The *coarse* grain of the wood makes it unsuitable for fine furniture.

這塊木頭粗糙的木紋,使其不適合用來做高級的傢俱。

coat 〔kot〕 *n.* 覆蓋在表面的一層(油漆等)

We will put a second *coat* of paint on the wall tomorrow.

我們明天將在這道牆上,漆上第二層油漆。

coated 〔'kotɪd〕 *adj.* 覆蓋著的

Each strawberry was *coated* with a thick layer of chocolate.

每顆草莓都被覆蓋上一層厚厚的巧克力。

cockpit 〔'kɑk,pɪt〕 *n.* (飛機的)駕駛艙

Soon after taking his place in the *cockpit*, the pilot took off. 那名飛行員進入駕駛艙就位後不久,就起飛了。

code 〔kod〕 *n.* 密碼

In order to send the message secretly, we will write it in *code*. 為了要秘密傳送這個訊息,我們將會以密碼書寫。

coil 〔kɔɪl〕 *v.* 將~捲起;捲繞成圈

The fisherman *coiled* the rope neatly and placed it on the deck of the boat.

漁夫很整齊地將繩子捲起,並把它放在漁船的甲板上。

collapse (kə'læps)
v. 倒塌

When the earthquake struck, several buildings *collapsed*.

當地震發生時，有好幾棟建築物倒塌。

col	+	lapse
together	+	*glide down*

collide (kə'laɪd) *v.*
相撞

Due to the foggy weather, the two cars *collided*.

由於濃霧的天氣，使得兩輛汽車相撞。

col	+	lide
together	+	*strike*

collision (kə'lɪʒən)
n. 相撞

The cause of the *collision* was careless driving.

這場相撞是由於開車不小心所引起的。

column ('kɑləm) *n.* 欄

The accountant added the *column* of figures twice because he was afraid of making a mistake.

那名會計將這欄的數字加了兩次，因為他害怕會出錯。

comedy ('kɑmədɪ)
n. 喜劇

We all enjoyed the *comedy* on TV last night so much that we couldn't stop laughing.

我們都非常喜歡昨天晚上電視播的那齣喜劇，以致於笑個不停。

comfortable

(ˈkʌmfətəbl̩) *adj.* 舒適的

This chair is the most *comfortable* one in the house.

這把椅子是屋裡最舒適的一把。

comfortably

(ˈkʌmfətəblɪ) *adv.* 舒服地

It is impossible to sleep *comfortably* on such a hard bed.

在這麼硬的床上，是不可能睡得舒服的。

comics (ˈkɑmɪkz)

n. pl. 連環漫畫

The *comics* are usually the favorite part of the newspaper for children.

報紙上的連環漫畫，通常是兒童最喜歡的部分。

command (kəˈmænd)

n. 命令

The sergeant gave the *command* to march. 這位中士下達行軍的命令。

```
com     + mand
 |          |
together with + order
```

commander

(kəˈmændɚ) *n.* 指揮官；
總司令

A *commander* in the navy holds an officer grade of five.

海軍總司令擁有五級的官階。

comment (ˈkɑnmɛnt)

v. 評論

The politician refused to *comment* on the issue.

這位政客拒絕評論這個議題。

commerce 〔'kɑmɝs 〕
n. 商業；貿易

Foreign *commerce* is an important part of the economy.
對外貿易是經濟中重要的一部份。

com	+ merce
together +	pay

commercial
〔 kə'mɝʃəl 〕 *adj.* 商業的

The military will no longer engage in *commercial* activities.
軍方將不再參與商業活動。

commission
〔 kə'mɪʃən 〕 *n.* 軍官的職務；軍官任命狀

The officer resigned his *commission*.
這位軍官辭去他的職務。

commit 〔 kə'mɪt 〕 *v.*
犯（罪）

The burglar promised that he would not *commit* any more crimes.
這名夜賊保證，不會再犯任何罪了。

communicate
〔 kə'mjunəˌket 〕 *v.* 溝通

He is a good speaker and can *communicate* well with everyone.
他是一位出色的演說者，能夠和每個人溝通得很好。

community
〔 kə'mjunətɪ 〕 *n.* 社區

Because the *community* is small, each person knows all the other members.
因為這個社區很小，所以每個人都認識其他所有的成員。

compact 〔 kəm'pækt 〕
adj. 小巧的

Although small, a *compact* car is very economical. 小型汽車雖然小，但非常省錢。

comparable

(′kampərəb!) *adj.* 比得
上的;類似的

The two products are *comparable* in every way but price, so we may as well buy the cheaper one.

這兩項產品除了價格以外,在各方面都很類似,所以我們不妨買較便宜的那個。

comparatively

(kəm′pærətɪvlɪ) *adv.*
相較之下

Comparatively, this apartment is the better of the two because it gets more light.

相較之下,這間公寓是兩間裡面較好的,因為它的採光較好。

compartment

(kəm′partmənt) *n.*
隔間

The many *compartments* in this suitcase will help you to keep your belongings organized.

這個行李箱有許多夾層,能幫助你將個人隨身物品弄得井然有序。

compass (′kʌmpəs)
n. 指南針

According to the *compass*, we are going west.

根據指南針顯示,我們正往西邊走。

compete (kəm′pit)
v. 競爭

During the tryouts, the basketball players will *compete* for the right to join the team. 在選拔賽中,籃球選手們要爭取加入該隊的權利。

competent
（'kɑmpətənt）*adj.* 能幹的

He is a *competent* cook and often prepares the family's dinner.
他很會做菜，常常爲全家人做晚餐。

complain （kəm'plen）
v. 抱怨

Students often *complain* about the quality of the food at school.
學生們常常抱怨學校食物的品質。

complete （kəm'plit）
adj. 完全的

Despite the severity of his illness, the patient was able to make a *complete* recovery.
儘管這個患者病得很重，但他還是能夠完全康復。

complex （kəm'plɛks）
adj. 複雜的

The students had difficulty solving the *complex* problem.
學生們很難解出這個複雜的問題。

complicate
（'kɑmplə,ket）*v.* 使複雜

I'm afraid your plan will only *complicate* the situation, not make it easier.
恐怕你的計劃只會使情況更複雜，而不是更容易。

complicated
（'kɑmplə,ketɪd）*adj.*
複雜的

The directions you gave me to the school were so *complicated* that I got lost. 你指引我到學校的路太複雜了，所以我就迷路了。

composite ﹙kəm'pɑzɪt﹚
adj. 綜合成的；混合成的

From the descriptions of several witnesses, police drew a *composite* picture of the suspect.

根據幾個目擊者的描述，警方畫出了嫌疑犯的綜合素描。

composition
﹙ˌkɑmpə'zɪʃən﹚ *n.* 構成；
混合物

The color green is a *composition* of blue and yellow.

綠色是藍色和黃色的混合。

compound
﹙kɑm'paʊnd﹚ *adj.* 複合的

Many English words are a *compound* of two words, for example, backyard.

很多英文字都是由兩個單字複合而成的，例如 backyard（後院）。

```
com  +  pound
 |        |
together +  put（放置）
```

compress ﹙kəm'prɛs﹚
v. 壓縮

If we *compress* these clothes, we will be able to close the suitcase.

如果我們將這些衣服壓緊一點，那就可以把行李箱關上了。

compulsory
﹙kəm'pʌlsərɪ﹚ *adj.* 強制的

Attending this class is *compulsory*. You may not miss any classes.

這堂課是一定要上的，你不可以翹課。

```
com + puls + ory
 |     |      |
with + drive + adj.
```

compute 〔kəm'pjut〕
v. 計算

A calculator can help us *compute* the total of several numbers.
計算機可以幫我們算出好幾個數字的總和。

computer
〔kəm'pjutɚ〕 *n.* 電腦

It is convenient to store information on a *computer*.
將資訊儲存在電腦中很方便。

conceal〔kən'sil〕*v.*
隱藏

The thief tried to *conceal* his weapon under his coat.
小偷試著把他的武器藏在外套下。

concentrate
〔'kɑnsṇ,tret〕*v.* 專心

I tried to study but found it difficult to *concentrate* on my books.
我試著要唸書，但發現我很難專注於課本。

con	+ centr	+ ate
together	+ center	+ v.

concern〔kən'sɝn〕
v. 與～有關   *n.* 關心

This discussion does not *concern* you. It is none of your business.
這個討論與你無關。不關你的事。

He showed his *concern* by taking the sick man to the doctor.
他把這名生病的男子送去看醫生，以表達他的關心。

concerning
〔kən'sɜnɪŋ〕 *prep.* 關於

The reporter asked the president several questions *concerning* the new policy.
記者詢問總統幾個有關新政策的問題。

concert〔'kɑnsɜt〕 *n.*
音樂會

The *concert* was a great success and the audience applauded the musicians.
這場音樂會非常成功，聽眾都為音樂家們鼓掌。

conclude〔kən'klud〕
v. 結束；下結論；推斷

I would like to *conclude* the meeting by thanking you all for your attention.
會議的最後，我要感謝各位專心聽講。

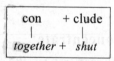

con   + clude
| |
together + shut

From his performance we can *conclude* that he is very talented.
我們可以從他的表現推斷出，他是很有才能的。

concrete〔'kɑnkrit〕
n. 水泥

The new bridge is made of *concrete* and is very strong.
這座新橋是以水泥建造的，所以十分堅固。

condense〔kən'dɛns〕
v. 濃縮

Can you *condense* your report to two pages? 你可以將報告濃縮成兩頁嗎？

com   + dense
| |
together + make thick

conduct 〔kən'dʌkt〕
v. 傳導

Be careful; the water will ***conduct*** the electric current.

小心一點，水是會導電的。

conductor
〔kən'dʌktɚ〕 *n.* 導體

Conductors are necessary in the production of electricity.

在發電時，必須要用到導體。

conference
〔'kɑnfərəns〕 *n.* 會議

Dr. Jones will represent the hospital at the medical ***conference*** next week.

瓊斯醫生將代表醫院，參加下星期的醫學會議。

confine 〔kən'faɪn〕
v. 限制；關起來

When the typhoon comes we may be ***confined*** to the house.

颱風來襲時，我們可能會被限制待在屋裡。

confirm 〔kən'fɝm〕
v. 確認

I called the airline to ***confirm*** my reservation.

我打電話到航空公司，確認我的訂位。

```
con   + firm
 |       |
wholly + firm
```

congratulate
〔kən'grætʃə,let〕 *v.* 恭喜

We will have a party tonight to ***congratulate*** him on his promotion.

我們今晚將舉辦一個派對，來恭賀他的升遷。

conscious ('kɑnʃəs)
adj. 刻意的；有意識的

If we make a *conscious* effort to work harder, I am sure we can finish the task on time.

如果我們刻意更加努力，我相信我們一定可以準時完成工作。

consequently
('kɑnsə,kwɛntlɪ) *adv.*
因此

He often eats junk food; *consequently*, he is overweight.

他常吃垃圾食物；因此他現在體重過重了。

considerable
(kən'sɪdərəb!) *adj.*
相當大的

Television has a *considerable* influence on people.

電視對人們有相當大的影響。

consist (kən'sɪst) *v.*
由～組成

Water *consists* of hydrogen and oxygen. 水是由氫和氧所組成的。

```
con    +  sist
 |         |
together + stand
```

constant ('kɑnstənt)
adj. 不斷的

His *constant* complaining irritates everyone. 他不斷的抱怨激怒了每個人。

construct
(kən'strʌkt) *v.* 建造

The government has decided to *construct* the new city hall on this site.

政府打算在這個地點，建造新的市政廳。

```
con    +  struct
 |         |
together + build
```

contact 〔'kɑntækt〕
v. 聯絡

Please *contact* me as soon as you arrive. 請你一到達，就和我聯絡。

con	+	tact
together	+	touch

contain 〔kən'ten〕 v.
包含；裝有

This jar *contains* glue and that one holds water.

這個廣口瓶裝的是膠水，而那個則是裝水。

contaminate
〔kən'tæmə,net〕 v.
污染；弄髒

A doctor must be careful not to *contaminate* his hands once he has washed them. 醫生一旦洗過手後，就必須小心不要再弄髒了。

con	+	tamin	+	ate
together	+	touch	+	v.

content 〔'kɑntɛnt〕 n.
內容

The *content* of the letter will not please you.

這封信的內容不會讓你高興的。

contest 〔'kɑntɛst〕 n.
比賽

The speech *contest* was difficult to judge because every student spoke well. 這場演講比賽很難評分，因為每個學生都講得很好。

continent
(ˈkɑntənənt) *n.* 洲;大陸

Spanish is spoken in most of the countries on the *continent* of South America.

南美洲大部分的國家,都說西班牙文。

continue (kənˈtɪnju)
v. 繼續

We are almost out of time. We can *continue* this discussion tomorrow.

我們快沒時間了。我們可以明天再繼續討論。

continuous
(kənˈtɪnjuəs) *adj.* 連續的

The resort's brochure promises *continuous* sunshine.

這個休閒勝地的介紹手冊,保證那邊的天氣會是持續的晴天。

contrast (kənˈtræst)
v. 使對比;使對照

In my report I will *contrast* the two proposals and then choose the better one. 我會在我的報告中比較這兩個提案,並選出較好的。

contra	+	st
against	+	stand

contribute
(kənˈtrɪbjut) *v.* 捐獻;
貢獻

We will all *contribute* some money to help pay for the graduation party.

我們所有人都會捐一些錢,來協助支付畢業舞會的費用。

con	+ tribute
together	+ bestow

convenient
〔kən'vinjənt〕 *adj.*
方便的

It is very *convenient* to take the bus to town; the bus stop is just across the street. 搭公車到城裡去非常方便；公車站就在對街。

converge〔kən'vɝdʒ〕
v. 集中於一點

If the lines are not parallel, they will eventually *converge*.
如果這些線是不平行的，那它們最後將會相交於一點。

convert〔kən'vɝt〕*v.*
轉變

Water will *convert* to steam when heated. 水在受熱時會轉變成蒸氣。

con	+	vert
together	+	turn

convinced
〔kən'vɪnst〕*adj.* 確信的

After seeing the latest poll, I am *convinced* that he will win the election.
看了最新的民調之後，我確信他會打贏選戰。

coordinate
〔ko'ɔrdn͵et〕*v.* 調整；
協調

The activities of the program are *coordinated* so as to make the best use of the limited time.
這個節目的活動被調整過了，以便善用有限的時間。

co	+	ordin	+	ate
with	+	order	+	v.

copper 〔ˈkɑpɚ〕 *n.* 銅

Copper is one of the metals that conduct electricity well.

銅是最會導電的金屬之一。

copy 〔ˈkɑpɪ〕 *n.* 影本
v. 影印

You had better make a *copy* of your report before you turn in the original.

在交出原版的報告之前,你最好先影印一份。

I have to *copy* my paper, but the machine is broken.

我必須影印我的報告,但機器故障了。

cord 〔kɔrd〕 *n.* 電線

The machine does not work because the power *cord* is not connected.

機器無法運作,因為電線沒接好。

core 〔kor〕 *n.* 中心

In some religions hell is located in the *core* of the Earth.

有些宗教主張,地獄是位於地球的中心。

corporal 〔ˈkɔrpərəl〕
n. 下士

A *corporal* holds a higher rank than a private does.

下士的官階高於二等兵。

correspond
〔ˌkɔrəˈspɑnd〕 *v.* 通信

When away from home, I *correspond* regularly with my family.

離家的時候,我會定期和家人通信。

corrode 〔kə'rod〕 v.
腐蝕；侵蝕

Salt will cause metal to *corrode* more quickly. 鹽會使金屬腐蝕得更快。

corrosion 〔kə'roʒən〕 *n.* 腐蝕；侵蝕

The rust on the car was evidence of *corrosion*. 車上的鐵鏽是腐蝕的證據。

counterclockwise
〔͵kautə'klɑk͵waɪz〕 *adj.*
逆時針方向的

You must turn a screw in a *counterclockwise* direction if you want to loosen it.
如果你想要將螺絲釘鬆開，那你必須要將它往逆時針方向旋轉。

countless 〔'kauntlɪs〕 *adj.* 無數的

There are a *countless* number of stars in the sky. 天空中有無數的星星。

courage 〔'kɝɪdʒ〕 *n.* 勇氣

Do you have the *courage* to jump out of a plane with a parachute?
你有沒有勇氣使用降落傘，從飛機上跳下來？

court 〔kort〕 *n.* 法院

Because the other driver refused to pay for the damage, we took him to *court* and asked the judge to settle it.
因為另一位駕駛人拒付損害的費用，所以我們帶他上法院，要求法官處理。

courtesy 〔'kɝtəsɪ〕 *n.* 禮貌

Saying "excuse me" is a sign of *courtesy*. 說「對不起」是種禮貌的表示。

crash 〔kræʃ〕 *n.* 墜毀

Miraculously, no one was killed in the plane *crash*.

不可思議的是，在這場墜機事件中，竟沒有造成任何人死亡。

crawl 〔krɔl〕 *v.* 爬

The soldiers had to *crawl* on their stomachs to get through the training course. 士兵們必須貼著地面爬行，來通過訓練課程。

crew 〔kru〕 *n.* 全體機員

The plane was carrying 100 passengers and a *crew* of seven. 這架飛機載了一百位乘客和七位機員。

crime 〔kraɪm〕 *n.* 罪

Murder is a very serious *crime*. 謀殺是很嚴重的罪。

criminal 〔ˈkrɪmənḷ〕 *n.* 罪犯

The defendant was a notorious *criminal* who had committed many crimes. 被告是個曾犯下多起案件，十分惡名昭彰的歹徒。

critical 〔ˈkrɪtɪkḷ〕 *adj.* 非常重要的

The entrance examination is a *critical* test for every student.

對每位學生而言，入學考試是個非常重要的考試。

criticism ('krɪtə,sɪzəm)
n. 批評

My teacher gave me some positive *criticism* of my writing style and it was very helpful.

老師對我的寫作風格提供一些正面的批評，對我很有幫助。

crop (krɑp) *n.* 農作物

Rice is an important *crop* in this country. 稻米是這個國家的重要農作物。

crosscheck ('krɔs,tʃɛk)
v. 核對；查證

We should *crosscheck* this information by looking at an independent study.

我們應該考察獨立的研究，來核對這項資料。

crush (krʌʃ) *v.* 壓碎

The car was *crushed* by the falling tree. 這輛汽車被倒下的樹給壓扁了。

cure (kjur) *n.* 治療法

Unfortunately, there is no *cure* for the common cold.

遺憾的是，一般的感冒是無藥可治的。

curious ('kjurɪəs) *adj.*
好奇的

Most students are *curious* about their classmates' scores.

大多數的學生，對於同學的分數都非常好奇。

curly ('kɜlɪ) *adj.* 捲曲的

Unlike her straight-haired sister, Jane has *curly* hair.

珍有一頭捲髮，不像她那直髮的姊姊。

currency ('kɜənsɪ)
n. 貨幣

When we travel abroad, we must change our money into local *currency*.

當我們到國外旅行時，必須把錢換成當地的貨幣。

current ('kɜənt) *n.*
電流

The electrical *current* is not stable here, so sometimes the lights will dim.

這裡的電流不穩，所以有時電燈會不亮。

curvature ('kɜvətʃə)
n. 彎曲；曲度

It is not easy to see the *curvature* of the earth with the naked eye.

用肉眼不容易看出地球的曲度。

custom ('kʌstəm) *n.*
習俗

It is a *custom* to bow when meeting people in Japan.

在日本，和人見面時鞠個躬，是一種習俗。

cycle ('saɪkḷ) *n.*
周期；循環

Death is an inevitable part of the life *cycle* of all living things.

死亡是所有生物在其生命周期中，無法避免的一部分。

D

data 〔 ˈdetə 〕 *n.pl.* 資料

It took him one hour to enter all the *data* into the computer.

他花了一小時，把所有的資料輸入電腦。

debt 〔 dɛt 〕 *n.* 債務

The national *debt* is the amount of money that the country owes.

國債就是國家所積欠的金額。

declare 〔 dɪˈklɛr 〕 *v.* 申報；宣佈

When you enter the country, a customs official will ask you to *declare* any restricted items, such as alcohol and cigarettes.

當你進入一個國家時，海關人員會要求你申報所有的限制物品，像是酒類和香煙。

```
de   + clare
 |       |
fully + clear
```

deflect 〔 dɪˈflɛkt 〕 *v.* 使轉向

The bullet was *deflected* by the metal door. 子彈碰到金屬門後，就轉變了方向。

defy 〔 dɪˈfaɪ 〕 *v.* 公然反抗

You will only make him angrier if you *defy* him.

如果你公然反抗他，只會使他更生氣。

```
de   +  fy
 |       |
apart + trust
```

delay ﹝ dɪ'le ﹞ v. 延期

We will ***delay*** the graduation ceremony until the rain stops.

我們會將畢業典禮，延到雨停之後再舉行。

demand ﹝ dɪ'mænd ﹞ n. v. 要求

The kidnapper had only one ***demand*** — one million dollars.

那名綁匪只有一個要求—— 一百萬元。

We believe the workers will ***demand*** a pay increase.

我們認爲，工人們會要求提高薪資。

demanding ﹝ dɪ'mændɪŋ ﹞ adj. 費力的；要求高的

A doctor has a very ***demanding*** job and often has no time to take a break.

醫生的工作是很費力的，而且常常沒有時間休息。

demonstrate ﹝'dɛmən,stret ﹞ v. 示範

She will ***demonstrate*** how to use the new computer program.

她將示範，要如何使用這個新的電腦程式。

denomination ﹝ dɪ,nɑmə'neʃən ﹞ n. 面額

The one dollar bill is the most common ***denomination*** of paper money in the United States.

一塊錢的鈔票，是美國最常見的紙鈔面額。

dense ﹝ dɛns ﹞ adj. 濃密的

The ***dense*** forest offers a lot of shade from the sun.

濃密的森林，提供了許多樹蔭來阻隔陽光。

density (ˈdɛnsətɪ) *n.*
密度

With the population *density* increasing, the city feels more crowded.
隨著人口密度逐漸增加，這個城市令人覺得更擁擠了。

dent (dɛnt) *n.* 凹痕

I put a *dent* in my car when I ran into that tree.
在我撞上那棵樹之後，我的車子就有了凹痕。

dental (ˈdɛntḷ) *adj.*
牙齒的

A toothache is a common *dental* problem. 牙痛是很常見的牙齒問題。

deny (dɪˈnaɪ) *v.* 拒絕
接受；否認

If you do not ask politely, the clerk will *deny* your request.
如果你不是很有禮貌地詢問，那名職員將拒絕接受你的要求。

department
(dɪˈpɑrtmənt) *n.* 部門

My sister works in the marketing *department* of the company.
我姊姊在那家公司的行銷部門上班。

dependable
(dɪˈpɛndəbḷ) *adj.* 可靠

I am sure she will do as she promised because she is very *dependable*.
我確定她會做到她所承諾的，因為她是個非常可靠的人。

dependent
(dɪˈpɛndənt) *adj.* 依賴的

Without his own car, he is *dependent* on public transportation. 他沒有自己的車，所以得依賴大眾運輸工具。

depress 〔dɪˊprɛs〕v.
降低；使沮喪

The economic slowdown will *depress* prices.

經濟發展減緩，將會使物價降低。

```
de   + press
 |      |
down + press
```

descend 〔dɪˊsɛnd〕v.
下降

The plane began to *descend* when it neared the airport.

飛機在靠近機場時，開始下降。

```
de   + scend
 |      |
down + climb
```

descent 〔dɪˊsɛnt〕n.
下降

The plane's *descent* was slow because of the bad weather.

因為天氣不好，所以飛機下降的速度緩慢。

desert 〔ˊdɛzət〕n. 沙漠

It is difficult to live in the *desert* because there is very little water.

在沙漠中很難生存，因為那裡的水很少。

designate 〔ˊdɛzɪɡ‚net〕
v. 指派

I have decided to *designate* Tom team captain. 我決定要指派湯姆當隊長。

desire 〔dɪˊzaɪr〕v. 想要

We can go wherever you *desire* for dinner.

我們可以到任何你想去的地方吃晚餐。

despite 〔dɪˊspaɪt〕prep.
不顧；儘管

She decided to buy the new car *despite* the cost.

她決定不計成本，買這輛新車。

destination

〔 ,dɛstə'neʃən 〕 *n.* 目的地

This bus will stop twice before reaching its final *destination*.

這輛公車在到達最終目的地之前，會停兩站。

destroy 〔 dɪ'strɔɪ 〕 *v.* 破壞

Too much rain may *destroy* the entire crop of corn. 過多的降雨量，可能會使整個玉米田的收成受到破壞。

destruction

〔 dɪ'strʌkʃən 〕 *n.* 破壞

The earthquake caused a lot of *destruction*. 地震造成了許多破壞。

detect 〔 dɪ'tɛkt 〕 *v.* 偵測

This radar can *detect* any moving object within 20 miles. 這個雷達可以偵測出，二十英哩內所有正在移動的物體。

```
de     +  tect
 |         |
away from + cover
```

determine 〔 dɪ'tɜmɪn 〕 *v.* 決定；確定

The professor considers many factors before he *determines* our final grades. 教授在決定我們最後的成績之前，考慮了許多因素。

With these test results, the doctor will be able to *determine* the cause of your illness. 有了這些測試結果，醫生就可以確定你的病因。

detonate

('dɛtə,net) v. 爆炸；
引爆

The soldier threw a grenade, but it did not *detonate*.

士兵丟出了一顆手榴彈，但並沒有爆炸。

We can *detonate* this bomb by remote control.

我們可以用遙控的
方式引爆炸彈。

de	+	ton	+ ate
down	+	thunder	+ v.

develop (dɪ'vɛləp)
v. 研發；發展

Doctors say they will *develop* a new vaccine by the end of the year. 醫生們說，
他們在年底之前，將會研發出一種新的疫苗。

deviate ('divɪ,et) v.
偏離

Although they could have taken a shortcut, the hikers decided not to *deviate* from their route. 雖然這些徒步旅行者可以走捷徑，但他們決定不要偏離他們的路線。

de	+	vi	+ ate
away from	+	way	+ v.

device (dɪ'vaɪs) n.
用具；裝置

A can opener is a very useful *device* for a cook. 開罐器對廚師而言，是很有用的用具。

diagonal

(daɪ'ægən!) adj. 對角
線的

Please draw a *diagonal* line from one corner of the rectangle to the opposite one. 請在長方形的一角，畫一條對角線到它的對角。

dai	+	gon	+	al
across	+	angle	+	adj.

diagram (ˈdaɪə‚græm)
n. 圖表;圖解

The mechanic studied the *diagram* of the engine before attempting to repair it.
機械工人在嘗試修理引擎之前,先研究了它的構造圖。

diesel (ˈdizl̩) *n.* 柴油

Most large trucks run on *diesel* fuel.
大多數的大卡車,都是以柴油當燃料。

differ (ˈdɪfɚ) *v.* 不同

The twins look identical, but they *differ* a great deal in personality.
這對雙胞胎看起來一模一樣,但他們的個性卻大不相同。

difference (ˈdɪfərəns)
n. 不同

It is difficult to tell the *difference* between the two brothers.
很難看出這兩兄弟的不同點。

dig (dɪg) *v.* 挖

The workers will *dig* a hole here for the new well.
工人們會在這裡挖個洞,來鑽新的井。

digest (daɪˈdʒɛst) *v.*
消化

It takes the body longer to *digest* meat than vegetables.
身體要消化肉類,得花比消化蔬菜類更長的時間。

digestion

(daɪˈdʒɛstʃən) *n.* 消化

It is said that tea is good for the *digestion*. 據說茶有助於消化。

digestive (daɪˈdʒɛstɪv)
adj. 消化的

The *digestive* system is what processes food.
消化系統是負責處理食物。

digit (ˈdɪdʒɪt) *n.* 阿拉伯數字（0~9 之中的一個）

1000 is the first four *digit* number.
一千是第一個四位數字。

dimensions

(dəˈmɛnʃənz) *n. pl.*
面積；大小

It is a large room with *dimensions* of 8 by 10 meters.
這個大房間的面積，是 8×10 平方公尺。

di	+	mension
apart	+	measure

dip (dɪp) *v.* 沾；浸

Some children like to *dip* their cookies in milk.
有些小孩喜歡把餅乾沾牛奶吃。

direct (dəˈrɛkt) *v.* 指引

Could you *direct* me to the post office?
你可以指引我到郵局去的路嗎？

dirt (dɜt) *n.* 泥土

The children were covered with *dirt* after playing in the garden.
孩子們在花園玩完後，全身沾滿泥土。

disadvantage

(ˌdɪsədˈvæntɪdʒ) *n.* 缺點

One *disadvantage* of living in the suburbs is having to commute to work.

要通勤去上班，是住在郊區的一個缺點。

disappoint

(ˌdɪsəˈpɔɪnt) *v.* 使失望

Although she was tired, Mary kept her promise to take the children to the park because she didn't want to *disappoint* them.

雖然瑪麗很累，她還是遵守諾言，帶孩子們到公園玩，因為她不想讓他們失望。

disaster (dɪzˈæstɚ)

n. 災害

An earthquake is an unpredictable natural *disaster*.

地震是一種不可預測的天然災害。

discard (dɪsˈkɑrd)

v. 丟棄

It is important to *discard* household trash in the proper way.

以適當方式丟棄家庭垃圾，是很重要的。

discharge (dɪsˈtʃɑrdʒ)

v. 使出院；發射

My uncle will be *discharged* from the hospital tomorrow.

我叔叔明天要出院。

Always put the safety on or you may *discharge* the gun accidentally.

一定要將槍枝上保險栓，否則你可能在無意中開槍。

discipline (ˈdɪsəplɪn)
v. 懲罰   *n.* 訓練;紀律

He was forced to *discipline* his son when he broke the rule.
當他的兒子犯規時,他被迫懲罰他。

Successful athletes have a great deal of *discipline*.
成功的運動員都接受大量的訓練。

disciplined
(ˈdɪsəplɪnd) *adj.* 遵守
紀律的

The *disciplined* piano student practices for two hours every day. 這個遵守紀律的學生,每天都會練兩小時的鋼琴。

discover (dɪˈskʌvɚ)
v. 發現

When Mr. Lee *discovered* that the students had cheated, he was very angry. 當李老師發現學生們作弊,他十分生氣。

discrepancy
(dɪˈskrɛpənsɪ) *n.* 矛盾

When the witness described what he had seen for the second time, the police discovered a *discrepancy* in his story.
當這個目擊者第二次描述他所看到的情景時,警方在他的敘述中發現了矛盾的地方。

```
dis  + crep + ancy
 |      |      |
apart + crack +  n.
```

disease (dɪˈziz) *n.*
疾病

Cancer is often a fatal *disease*.
癌症常是致命的疾病。

diseased〔dɪ'zizd〕
adj. 生病的

The farmer cut down the tree because it was *diseased*.
因爲這棵樹生病了，所以農夫將它砍下來。

dishonest〔dɪs'ɑnɪst〕
adj. 不誠實的

Telling lies is *dishonest* behavior.
說謊是不誠實的行爲。

dishwasher
〔'dɪʃ,wɑʃɚ〕 *n.* 洗碗機

The new apartment has many conveniences, including a *dishwasher*.
新的公寓有許多便利的設備，其中包括洗碗機。

disk〔dɪsk〕*n.* 磁片

The computer program is stored on this *disk*. 這個電腦程式是存在這張磁片裡。

dismiss〔dɪs'mɪs〕*v.*
下（課）；解散

The teacher decided to *dismiss* the class early because a dangerous storm was coming. 因爲有個危險的暴風雨即將來臨，所以老師決定提早下課。

```
dis  + miss
 |       |
away + send
```

dismissal〔dɪs'mɪsḷ〕
n. 免職；解僱

I think Joe's *dismissal* was unfair because he always did a good job and was never late for work.
我覺得喬被免職是很不公平的，因爲他總是把工作做好，而且上班從不遲到。

```
dis  + miss + al
 |      |      |
apart + throw + n.
```

dismount〔 dɪs'maʊnt 〕
v. 下（車）

Paul had to *dismount* his bicycle and walk down the street because it was crowded with shoppers.

保羅必須從自行車上下來，並順著街道走下去，因為街道擠滿了購物者。

```
dis    + mount
 |        |
negative + ascend
```

displace〔 dɪs'ples 〕
v. 強迫遷離

The new highway will *displace* about 30 families, but the government has promised to help them find new homes. 新的公路要強迫遷離大約三十戶人家，但是政府保證會協助他們找到新家。

display〔 dɪ'sple 〕*n.*
展覽；展示

There is an interesting *display* of pottery at the museum.
博物館正展出一場有趣的陶器展。

dispose〔 dɪ'spoz 〕*v.*
處置 <*of*>

What is the proper way to *dispose* of an old battery?
要處置舊電池，用什麼方法才正確呢？

disregard
〔 ˌdɪsrɪ'gard 〕*v.* 不顧；
不理

If you *disregard* the doctor's advice, you will not get well.
如果你不顧醫生的忠告，你就不會康復。

dissolve ﹝ dɪ'zɑlv ﹞ v.
溶解

The sugar *dissolved* quickly in the hot tea.　糖很快地就溶解在熱茶中。

distinct ﹝ dɪ'stɪŋkt ﹞
adj. 明顯的；不同的

There is a *distinct* difference between these two books.
這兩本書有很明顯的不同。

A musical scale is made up of seven *distinct* notes.
音階是由七個不同的音符所組成。

distinguish
﹝ dɪ'stɪŋgwɪʃ ﹞ v. 辨別

It is easy to *distinguish* between apples and oranges.
蘋果和柳橙很容易辨別。

distinguished
﹝ dɪ'stɪŋgwɪʃt ﹞ adj.
著名的；卓越的

Everyone is eager to meet the *distinguished* writer.
每個人都渴望見到這位名作家。

He was *distinguished* for his work in science.
他在科學上的工作表現十分傑出。

distort ﹝ dɪs'tɔrt ﹞ v.
使變形

Too much damp weather may *distort* the wooden door and then it will not close properly.
太潮濕的天氣會使木門變形，如此一來，門就沒辦法關好。

distract ﹝ dɪˋstrækt ﹞
v. 使分心

The sound of the television will *distract* me from my studies.
電視的聲音會使我從課業上分心。

distribute
﹝ dɪˋstrɪbjut ﹞ v. 分配

Some firms *distribute* bonuses to their employees at the end of the year.
有些公司在年底會分
配紅利給員工。

dis	+	tribute
apart	+	give

district ﹝ˋdɪstrɪkt ﹞ n.
區域

This *district* of the city is very popular now because of the new transportation system. 在這個城市裡,這個區域現在非常受歡迎,因為有新的運輸系統。

disturb ﹝ dɪˋstɝb ﹞ v.
打擾

Please don't *disturb* me while I am studying.
請不要在我唸書的時候打擾我。

dive ﹝ daɪv ﹞ v. 跳水

A crowd gathered to watch the man *dive* from the cliff into the sea below.
有一群人聚集在一起,看那名男子從懸崖上跳進底下的海裡。

divorce ﹝ dəˋvors ﹞
n. v. 離婚

The boy is upset because his parents are getting a *divorce*.
這男孩感到心煩,因為他的父母快離婚了。

document
('dɑkjəmənt) *n.* 文件

It is a good idea to keep important *documents* like your passport in a safe place.
將像護照這樣的重要文件收在安全的地方，是個好主意。

dorm (dɔrm) *n.* 宿舍

The freshmen are required to live in the school *dorm*. 這些大一新鮮人被要求得住在學校的宿舍。

double ('dʌbḷ) *adj.*
雙倍的

Hoping to feel better sooner, he took a *double* dose of the medicine.
爲了希望早點康復，他服用了雙倍劑量的藥。

doubtful ('daʊtfəl)
adj. 不大可能的

It is *doubtful* that Joan will come to the party; she wasn't feeling well this morning. 瓊恩不大可能會參加派對，因爲她今天早上身體不太舒服。

drain (dren) *v.* 抽乾；
排乾

The university will *drain* the swimming pool for the winter.
大學在冬天會把游泳池的水抽乾。

drama ('drɑmə) *n.*
戲劇

"Meteor Garden" is a popular TV *drama*.
「流星花園」是很受歡迎的電視劇。

draw 〔 drɔ 〕*v.* 拉;拖;吸引

The tide *drew* the boat out to sea.
潮水將船拖向海中。

The new exhibition is expected to *draw* a lot of people to the museum.
這場新的展覽預期會吸引很多人到博物館來。

dread 〔 drɛd 〕*v.* 恐懼;害怕

He *dreads* going to the doctor because he doesn't like to take medicine.
因為他不喜歡吃藥,所以害怕去看醫生。

drift 〔 drɪft 〕*v.* 漂流

We turned off the engine and let the boat *drift* in the water.
我們將引擎關掉,讓船隻在水中漂流。

drill 〔 drɪl 〕*v.* 嚴格叫人反覆練習 *n.* 鑽孔機

Our English teacher often *drills* us in the new sentence patterns. 我們英文老師常常要我們反覆練習新的句型。

drown 〔 draʊn 〕*v.* 淹死;溺水

Many people *drown* in this river every year because of the strong current.
每年都有許多人在這條水流強勁的河裡淹死。

drug 〔 drʌg 〕*n.* 藥

You must have a doctor's prescription in order to buy this *drug*.
為了買這種藥,你必須要有醫生開的處方。

drum 〔 drʌm 〕 *n.* 鼓

My son plays the *drums* in the school band. 我兒子在學校的樂團打鼓。

dryer 〔'draɪɚ 〕 *n.* 烘乾機

It is much more convenient to wash clothes with your own washer and *dryer*.

用你自己的洗衣機和烘乾機來清洗衣服，方便多了。

dual 〔'djuəl 〕 *adj.* 二的；雙重的

The actor played a *dual* role in the movie.

這位男演員在這部電影中分飾兩角。

```
du  +  al
 |      |
two  +  adj.
```

due 〔 dju 〕 *adj.* 應付的；到期的

The rent is *due* at the end of the month. 房租月底到期了。

dumb 〔 dʌm 〕 *adj.* 愚蠢的

Don't think you are too *dumb* to understand the math lesson; just listen carefully.

不要覺得你太笨，無法理解數學課程；你只要專心聽講就可以了。

duty 〔'djutɪ 〕 *n.* 責任；義務

Cooking dinner is one of the housekeeper's *duties*.

做晚飯是家庭主婦的責任之一。

dye 〔 daɪ 〕 v. 染

We decided to *dye* the curtains yellow in order to make the room look brighter.

為了要讓房間看起來較為明亮，我們決定要把窗簾染成黃色的。

dynamite

〔'daɪnə,maɪt 〕 n. 炸藥

Dynamite is often used in mining and in other industries where great amounts of rock must be moved.

炸藥常常被用在採礦業和其他工業，因為這些行業常需要搬動大量的石塊。

【劉毅老師的話】

　　將背不下來的單字作一記號，複習的時候，想辦法把它記下來。如：dye 這個字背不下來，知道它的同音字是 die，比較兩者的不同，就容易記了。

E

eager 〔'igə〕 *adj.* 渴望的

Everyone is *eager* to hear the results of the election.
每個人都渴望聽到選舉的結果。

ease 〔iz〕 *n.* 輕鬆；悠閒

The strong man carried the heavy box with *ease*. 這個強壯的男人輕鬆地就把這個沉重的箱子抬起來。

The soldiers were allowed to stand at *ease* while the sergeant spoke.
士兵們被允許在士官說話時，保持稍息的姿勢。

echo 〔'εko〕 *n.* 回音

If we shout in the cave, we will hear our *echo* a moment later. 如果我們在洞穴中大叫，過一會兒，就會聽到回音。

economy 〔ɪ'kɑnəmɪ〕 *n.* 經濟

The *economy* of the country is stable and attracts a lot of investors.
這個國家的經濟狀況很穩定，吸引了許多投資者。

editor 〔'εdɪtə〕 *n.* 編輯

The *editor* decided not to print the story because it was not supported by solid proof.
因為沒有可靠的證據來證明這個故事，所以編輯決定不出版它。

educational
〔͵ɛdʒʊ'keʃənḷ〕*adj.* 教育的

His *educational* background is outstanding; he graduated from one of the top schools.
他的學歷很不錯；他畢業於一所頂尖的學校。

effect〔ə'fɛkt , ɪ'fɛkt〕
n. 效果；影響

I took the medicine, but it did not have any *effect* on my illness.
我吃了藥，但對我的病沒有任何效果。

effective〔ə'fɛktɪv〕
adj. 有效的

The advertising campaign was very *effective* in attracting new customers.
這個廣告宣傳活動非常有效，能吸引新的顧客。

efficiency〔ə'fɪʃənsɪ〕
n. 效率

Efficiency is essential in the business world. 效率在商業界是非常重要的。

efficient〔ə'fɪʃənt〕
adj. 有效率的

The new worker is very *efficient* and always completes the work ahead of schedule.
新來的工人十分有效率，而且總是提前完成工作。

effort〔'ɛfət〕*n.* 努力

The workers made an *effort* to finish the job on time.
工人們努力準時將工作完成。

either 〔'iðɚ〕 *adv.*
不是…（就是～）

I didn't buy any shoes at that store because they were all *either* too expensive or too old-fashioned.

我沒有在那家店買任何鞋子，因為它們不是太貴，就是樣式過時。

elastic 〔ɪ'læstɪk〕 *adj.*
有彈性的

Clothes with an *elastic* waistband can be worn by people of different sizes.

附彈性腰帶的衣服，可以給不同身材的人穿。

elderly 〔'ɛldɚlɪ〕 *adj.*
年老的

The boy helped his *elderly* grandfather cross the busy street.

這個男孩扶他年老的祖父，穿越這條熱鬧的街道。

elect 〔ɪ'lɛkt〕 *v.* 選舉

We *elect* a new president every year in the astronomy club.

我們天文學社，每年都會選一位新的社長。

electric 〔ɪ'lɛktrɪk〕
adj. 電的

Be careful not to touch a bare wire or you may receive an *electric* shock.

小心不要去碰到沒有遮蓋的電線，否則你會遭受電擊。

electrical 〔ɪ'lɛktrɪkl̩〕
adj. 電的

We need *electrical* power in order to run this machine.

我們需要電力來運作這台機器。

electrician
(ɪ,lɛk'trɪʃən) *n.* 電工

We called in an *electrician* to look at the wiring. 我們找了一位電工來看一下配線。

electricity
(ɪ,lɛk'trɪsətɪ) *n.* 電

The rent includes all utilities except *electricity*.
房租包含所有的公共設施，除了電力之外。

electrode
(ɪ'lɛktrod)
n. 電極

The current enters the circuit through this *electrode* and exits through the other. 電流從迴路的這一極進入，然後從另外一極流出。

electron (ɪ'lɛktrɑn)
n. 電子

All *electrons* have a negative charge.
所以的電子都含有負電荷。

electronics
(ɪ,lɛk'trɑnɪks) *n.*
電子學

You should not try to repair this equipment yourself unless you have some knowledge of *electronics*.
你不該自己試著修理這個設備，除非你有一些電子學方面的知識。

element ('ɛləmənt)
n. 要素；元素

Sodium chloride is made up of two *elements*.
氯化鈉（食鹽）是由兩種元素所組成的。

elevate ('ɛlə,vet) *v.*
提昇

Your test score is high enough to *elevate* you to the next level.
你的考試成績已經夠高了，足以將你提升到下一個等級了。

emission 〔 ɪ'mɪʃən 〕
n. 排氣

The new *emission* system in these cars may reduce pollution by 25%.
這些車裡的新型排氣系統，可能會減少百分之二十五的污染量。

emit 〔 ɪ'mɪt 〕 *v.* 發出

The speaker *emits* a loud, high-pitched sound when there is a fire.
失火時，擴音器會發出大而尖銳的聲音。

emphasis 〔'ɛmfəsɪs 〕
n. 重點；強調

Let's place the most *emphasis* on the work that needs to be completed first.
我們將重點放在必須最先完成的工作上吧。

enable 〔 ɪn'ebḷ 〕 *v.*
使能夠

This dictionary will *enable* you to find out the meaning of any word you don't know. 這本字典可以使你找到任何你不懂的單字的意思。

encircle 〔 ɪn's₃kḷ 〕 *v.*
環繞；包圍

Trees *encircle* the house, hiding it from view. 群樹環繞，使這棟房子被隱藏在別人看不見的地方。

enclose 〔 ɪn'kloz 〕 *v.*
包圍；隨函附寄

A fence *enclosed* the pasture, preventing the animals from running away.
牧場周圍有籬笆圍著，以防止動物逃走。

I *enclosed* a check for the tuition in my letter to the school.
我將付學費的支票，附在我寄給學校的信中。

encounter

〔 ɪn'kaʊntɚ 〕 *v.* 遇見

We did not expect to *encounter* him at the meeting yesterday.

我們沒有想到會在昨天的會議上遇見他。

encourage〔 ɪn'kɝɪdʒ 〕

v. 鼓勵

My friends always *encourage* me to try my best.

我的朋友們總是鼓勵我要盡力。

endanger〔 ɪn'dendʒɚ 〕

v. 危害

A careless driver will not only *endanger* himself but others on the road as well. 粗心的駕駛人，不但會危害自己，也會危及路上其他的人。

endorse〔 ɪn'dɔrs 〕*v.*

背書；支持

A witness must *endorse* your will in order for it to be legal.

必須要有一個證人替你的遺囑背書，你的遺囑才算合法。

```
en + dorse
 |     |
in + back
```

I cannot *endorse* him for the position of treasurer because I believe he is dishonest. 我無法支持他擔任財務主管這個職位，因為我認為他並不誠實。

endure〔 ɪn'djʊr 〕*v.*

忍受

I closed the window because I cannot *endure* the traffic noise.

我將窗戶關上，因為我無法忍受交通的噪音。

energy (ˈɛnədʒɪ) *n.*
精力

She put all her *energies* into raising her three children.

她把全部的精力用於養育她的三個小孩。

```
en  +  erg  + y
|       |      |
into + work +  n.
```

enforce (ɪnˈfors) *v.*
執行；實施

The police find it difficult to *enforce* such a vague law.

警方覺得要執行這樣一條模糊的法律是很困難的。

enlist (ɪnˈlɪst) *v.* 從軍

Jimmy plans to *enlist* in the army after he graduates from high school.

吉米打算在高中畢業後就去從軍。

enlisted man
(ɪnˈlɪstɪd‚mæn) *n.* 士兵

My brother is an *enlisted man* and he just finished his basic training.

我哥哥是一名士兵，他剛剛完成基本訓練。

enough (əˈnʌf) *adv.*
足夠地

The carpet is large *enough* to cover the entire floor of this room.

這塊地毯大到足以覆蓋整個房間的地板。

ensign (ˈɛnsaɪn) *n.* 少尉

The rank of an *ensign* is below that of a lieutenant.

少尉的階級比中尉低。

ensure (ɪnˈʃʊr) v. 確保

The candidate's fame helped to *ensure* his success in the election.

這位候選人的名聲，有助於確保他在這場選舉的成功。

enter (ˈɛntɚ) v. 進入

When the teacher *enters* the classroom, you should stand up.

當老師走進教室，你們應該要起立。

enthusiasm
(ɪnˈθjuzɪˌæzəm) n.
熱忱；狂熱

Bill has a lot of *enthusiasm* for the project and can't wait to get started.

比爾對這個計劃案有很大的熱忱，他等不及要開始進行了。

entire (ɪnˈtaɪr) adj.
整個的

We ate the *entire* cake last night. There is nothing left.

我們昨晚將整個蛋糕都吃光了。一點都不剩。

entrance (ˈɛntrəns)
n. 入口

The *entrance* to the store is around the corner, on the side of the building.

這家店的入口在轉角附近，也就是在這棟建築物的側面。

entry (ˈɛntrɪ) n. 入口

The *entry* to this building is well guarded.

這棟建築物的入口處戒備森嚴。

environment
〔 ɪnˈvaɪrənmənt 〕 n. 環境

Industrial pollution may harm the
environment. 工業污染可能會危害環境。

en + viron + ment
| | |
in + *circuit* +   *n.*

equally 〔ˈikwəlɪ 〕
adv. 相等地；同樣地

The parents love all of their children
equally.
父母對他們所有小孩的愛都是同樣的。

equator 〔 ɪˈkwetɚ 〕
n. 赤道

Countries located on the ***equator***
usually have a tropical climate.
位於赤道上的國家，通常有熱帶性氣候。

equip 〔 ɪˈkwɪp 〕 *v.*
使配備；裝備

The team will ***equip*** the players with
uniforms, but they must provide their
own shoes.
隊上會為球員配有制服，但他們必須準備
自己的鞋子。

equipment
〔 ɪˈkwɪpmənt 〕 *n.* 設備；
器材

Tim likes to use the exercise
equipment at the gym.
提姆喜歡使用健身房裡的運動設備。

equivalent
〔 ɪˈkwɪvələnt 〕 *adj.*
相等的

One US dollar is ***equivalent*** to 130
Japanese yen today.
今天一塊錢美金等於一百三十塊日圓。

erect〔ɪ'rɛkt〕*v.* 豎立；
建造

We plan to *erect* a building here to house the new library.

我們打算在這裡建一棟新的建築物，作爲新圖書館的地點。

erratic〔ə'rɛtɪk〕*adj.*
不規則的

The police made the driver stop because his driving was *erratic*. He was driving all over the road.

警方要這位駕駛人停車，因爲他開車很不規則。他的車橫行整條馬路。

escape〔ə'skep〕*v.*
逃脫；逃走

Fortunately, all of the passengers were able to *escape* the burning plane.

幸運的是，所有乘客都能逃離那架起火燃燒的飛機。

especially〔ə'spɛʃəlɪ〕
adv. 特別地

The suit was made *especially* for Peter, so it fits him perfectly. 這套西裝是特別爲彼得做的，所以非常適合他。

essential〔ə'sɛnʃəl〕
adj. 必要的；重要的

It is *essential* that you follow the directions exactly, or the machine will break down. 你必須很確實地遵照說明書的指示，否則機器會故障。

evaluate〔ɪ'væljʊ,et〕
v. 評估

This test will help me to *evaluate* your progress.

這項測試可以幫助我評估你的進步情況。

evaporate
〔 ɪ'væpə,ret 〕 v. 蒸發

Water will *evaporate* when it is heated.
水被加熱後會蒸發。

event 〔 ɪ'vɛnt 〕 n. 事件

The prince's wedding was called the
event of the year.
王子的婚禮被稱爲是年度大事。

eventually
〔 ɪ'vɛntʃʊəlɪ 〕 adv. 最後

John saved a little money each month
and was *eventually* able to buy the
car he wanted.   約翰每個月都存一點錢，
最後他就能買他想要的那部車。

evident 〔'ɛvədənt 〕
adj. 明顯的

It is *evident* that you studied very hard
because you got a high score on the
exam. 顯然你非常用功唸書，因爲你在考
試中得到很高的分數。

e + vid + ent
| | |
out + see + adj.

examine 〔 ɪg'zæmɪn 〕
v. 檢查

The nurse asked me to wait here until
the doctor comes to *examine* me.
護士要我在這裡等，直到醫生來爲我做
檢查。

exceed 〔 ɪk'sid 〕 v.
超過

If you *exceed* the speed limit, you will
have to pay a heavy fine.
如果你超過速限，你將必
須支付大筆的罰款。

ex + ceed
| |
out + go

excess 〔 ɪk'sɛs 〕 *n.*
超過;多餘

There was an *excess* of food at the banquet and the manager decided to give it to the poor.
宴會中有剩下的食物,經理決定要將它送給窮人。

excessive 〔 ɪk'sɛsɪv 〕
adj. 過度的

Your worry about this exam is *excessive*. I'm sure that you'll do well.
你對這個考試擔心過度了,我確定你會考得很好。

exclude 〔 ɪk'sklud 〕
v. 排除

I would like to *exclude* the results of this experiment from the study because I believe they are not correct.
我想把這次實驗的結果自研究中刪除,因為我認為那些是不正確的。

```
ex + clude
 |      |
out +  shut
```

The rent includes all utilities, *excluding* telephone service. You will have to pay for that yourselves.
房租包含所有水電瓦斯等費用,但不含電話費。你比須自己付電話費。

exert 〔 ɪg'zɝt 〕 *v.* 努力

You must *exert* yourself if you want to finish the work on time.
如果你想準時完成工作,就必須靠自己努力。

exhale 〔 εks'hel 〕 *v.*
吐氣

When you hold your breath, you do not
exhale. 當你屏住呼吸時，你不能吐氣。

```
ex  +  hale
|       |
out + breathe
```

exhaust 〔 ɪg'zɔst 〕 *v.*
用盡；使筋疲力盡

We have *exhausted* the supply of fuel
and must buy some more.
燃料的存量已經用盡，我們必須再買一些。

You shouldn't work outside all day;
you will *exhaust* yourself.
你不應該在外面工作一整天，你會累壞自己。

exhibit 〔 ɪg'zɪbɪt 〕 *v.*
展出

The museum will *exhibit* the new
pieces next month.
博物館下個月將展出一批新的畫。

exist 〔 ɪg'zɪst 〕 *v.* 存在

Human beings did not *exist* when
dinosaurs roamed the earth.
當恐龍在地球上漫步時，人類並不存在。

exit 〔 'εgzɪt 〕 *n.* 出口

The theater has four *exits* so people
can leave it quickly.
這家戲院有四個出口，所以人們可以很快
地離去。

```
ex  +  it
|      |
out + go
```

expel 〔 ɪk'spɛl 〕 v. 驅逐

If you break any more rules, we will be forced to *expel* you from school.

如果你再犯規，我們將被迫將你逐出學校。

ex + pel
| |
out + drive

experience
〔 ɪk'spɪrɪəns 〕 n. 經驗

The doctor has more than twenty years of *experience*.

這位醫生有超過二十年的經驗。

experiment
〔 ɪk'spɛrəmənt 〕 n. 實驗

The result of the *experiment* helped to prove the scientist's theory.

實驗的結果有助於證明這位科學家的理論。

explode 〔 ɪk'splod 〕
v. 爆炸

Soon after the fuse is lit, the dynamite will *explode*.

引信點燃後不久，炸藥就會爆炸。

explosive 〔 ɪk'splosɪv 〕
n. 爆裂物；炸藥

Dynamite is a common *explosive*.

炸藥是一種常見的爆裂物。

export 〔 ɪks'port 〕 v.
出口

Several countries in the Middle East *export* oil.

有幾個中東國家出口石油。

express 〔 ɪk'sprɛs 〕 *v.*
表達

When the speaker finished, he invited the audience to *express* their opinions.
當演講者講完後，他請聽衆發表自己的意見。

extend 〔 ɪk'stɛnd 〕 *v.*
延長；擴張

I would like to stay longer, but it is impossible for me to *extend* my vacation.
我想待久一點，但是又不可能把假期延長。

extension 〔 ɪk'stɛnʃən 〕
n. 延期；附加；分機

I did not finish my report on time, but my professor gave me an *extension*.
我沒有準時完成我的報告，但是教授讓我延期。

extensive 〔 ɪk'stɛnsɪv 〕
adj. 大規模的；大量的

It requires *extensive* training to become an engineer.
要成爲工程師，需要接受大量的訓練。

extent 〔 ɪk'stɛnt 〕 *n.*
程度；範圍

I agree with your idea to some *extent*, but I cannot give it my complete approval.
就某種程度而言，我同意你的想法，但我無法完全贊同。

extinguish
〔 ɪk'stɪŋkwɪʃ 〕 v. 熄滅

The waiter asked us to *extinguish* our cigarettes because we were in the nonsmoking section.
服務生要求我們把香煙熄掉，因為我們坐在非吸煙區。

extreme〔 ɪk'strim 〕
adj. 極端的

The *extreme* heat in the desert made everyone uncomfortable.
沙漠中的酷熱讓每個人都不舒服。

extremely〔 ɪk'strimlɪ 〕
adv. 極度地

The *extremely* heavy rains nearly destroyed the bridge.
極大的雨勢幾乎毀了這座橋。

eyesight〔 'aɪ,saɪt 〕 n.
視力

It is said that watching too much television can damage your *eyesight*.
聽說看太多電視會傷害你的視力。

【劉毅老師的話】

　　利用「字根字源分析法」背單字，速度可加快三倍，如：

auto｜bio｜graphy　（自傳）
自己｜一生｜記錄

F

facility (fə'sɪlətɪ) *n.*
設施

The cafeteria is a new *facility*. It was built last year.
自助餐廳是新的設施，它是去年才建的。

factor ('fæktɚ) *n.* 因素

The weather was a *factor* in the accident.
天氣是造成這場意外的因素之一。

failure ('feljɚ) *n.*
不足；故障

The machine would not start because there was an electrical *failure*.
這台機器無法啓動，因爲電力不足。

faint (fent) *v.* 昏倒

She said she would *faint* if she did not eat something soon.
她說如果她不馬上吃點東西，就會昏倒。

fair (fɛr) *adj.* 晴朗的；
公平的

It is *fair* today but rain is expected tomorrow.
今天天氣晴朗，但明天預計會下雨。

The referee was very *fair*; he treated both teams in the same way.
裁判非常公平，他以同樣的方式對待兩隊。

fairly ('fɛrlɪ) *adv.*
相當地

The apartment is *fairly* close to the park. 這間公寓離公園很近。

faith ﹝ feθ ﹞ *n.* 信任；
信心

My little sister still has *faith* in Santa Claus.
我的小妹妹還是相信有聖誕老公公的存在。

I know you can do it; I have *faith* in you.
我知道你可以辦到，我對你有信心。

familiar ﹝ fə'mɪljə ﹞
adj. 熟悉的

I don't know where the post office is because I am not *familiar* with this town.
我不知道郵局在哪裡，因為我對這個城鎮不熟悉。

fare ﹝ fɛr ﹞ *n.* 車資；票價

The airline is offering a special *fare* from London to Paris.
這家航空公司正提供從倫敦到巴黎的特惠票價。

farm ﹝ farm ﹞ *n.* 農場

The *farm* produces corn, potatoes and other vegetables.
這座農場出產玉米、馬鈴薯，和其他蔬菜。

farmer ﹝'farmə ﹞ *n.*
農夫

My uncle left his life in the city to become a *farmer*.
我叔叔離開城市的生活，成為一位農夫。

fatal ('fetl) *adj.* 致命的

The doctor says that she has a *fatal* illness and has only a few weeks to live. 醫生說她得了不治之症,只剩幾個星期可活。

favor ('fevɚ) *n.* 恩惠;幫忙

Please do me a *favor* and copy this report for me.
請幫我一個忙,替我影印這份報告。

fear (fɪr) *n.* 恐懼
v. 害怕

He does not like to stand on the roof because he has a *fear* of heights.
他不喜歡站在屋頂,因為他有懼高症。

They *fear* the swimming class because they are afraid of water.
他們很怕上游泳課,因為他們會怕水。

feature ('fitʃɚ) *n.* 特色

Individual instruction is a *feature* of the course.
個別教導是這門課的一個特色。

female ('fimel) *adj.* 雌的;母的

A *female* cow is more docile than a bull. 母牛比公牛要溫順多了。

fertile ('fɝtl) *adj.* 肥沃的

The *fertile* soil produced a good crop of rice. 這些肥沃的土壤能出產優質的稻米作物。

fert	+	ile
bear	+	*adj.* (易於結果實的)

fight 〔 faɪt 〕 v. 打架

There is no need to *fight* over the last cookie; there are more in the cupboard.
沒有必要為了最後一塊餅乾打架；櫥櫃裡還有。

file 〔 faɪl 〕 v. 將…歸檔

The doctor *files* his patients' records in alphabetical order.
醫生將病人的紀錄依照字母序歸檔。

fill 〔 fɪl 〕 v. 填寫；配（藥方）

The pharmacist said he would *fill* the prescription right away.
藥劑師說他會馬上按處方配藥。

filling 〔'fɪlɪŋ 〕 n. 填補；補牙

The dentist suggested that I get a *filling* before the cavity got any worse.
牙醫師建議我，在蛀牙惡化之前先補牙。

firearm 〔'faɪr͵arm 〕 n. 武器

The guard carries a *firearm* at all times. 守衛隨時攜帶著武器。

firm 〔 fɝm 〕 adj. 堅固的

The building collapsed because it was not built on a *firm* foundation.
這棟建築物倒塌了，因為沒有蓋在堅固的地基上。

first-class 〔'fɝst͵klæs 〕 adj. 頭等車廂或艙位的

The tourists had seats in the *first-class* carriage of the train.
這些觀光客的座位在火車的頭等車廂裡。

fit〔fɪt〕*adj.* 健康的

Jogging is a good way to stay *fit*.
慢跑是保持健康的好方法。

fitness〔'fɪtnɪs〕*n.* 健康

One month after starting the *fitness* program he felt healthier and more energetic.
在開始健身課程一個月後，他覺得更健康，而且更有活力了。

fixed〔fɪkst〕*adj.* 固定的

The date of the graduation ceremony has been *fixed* and it will not be changed for any reason.
畢業典禮的日期已經確定了，不會因為任何理由而改變。

flag〔flæg〕*n.* 旗子

In most countries the national flag is *flown* in front of government buildings. 在大多數國家，政府機關的前面，都會懸掛國旗。

flame〔flem〕*n.* 火焰

The *flame* of the candle was unsteady in the wind. 蠟燭的火焰在風中搖晃。

flammable
〔'flæməbl̩〕*adj.* 易燃的

Because the storage building was filled with a lot of *flammable* materials, it burned quickly.
因為倉儲大樓堆了許多易燃的材料，所以很快就燒起來了。

flap 〔 flæp 〕 *n.* 機翼

The pilot adjusted the *flaps* of the airplane when he began his descent.
當飛機開始降落時，飛行員調整了一下機翼。

flashlight 〔 'flæʃ,laɪt 〕 *n.* 手電筒

We had to depend on *flashlights* when the power was cut off.
斷電時，我們必須依賴手電筒。

flavor 〔 'flevɚ 〕 *n.* 味道；口味

Strawberry is my favorite *flavor* of ice cream.
草莓是我最喜歡的冰淇淋口味。

flaw 〔 flɔ 〕 *n.* 裂縫；瑕疵

We had to replace the window because there was a *flaw* in the glass.
我們必須要換窗戶，因為玻璃上有個裂縫。

fleet 〔 flit 〕 *n.* 艦隊；船隊

The *fleet* will set sail in the morning.
艦隊將在早晨啟航。

flexible 〔 'flɛksəbḷ 〕 *adj.* 有彈性的；柔順的

The plastic is *flexible* so it will bend rather than break. 塑膠製品因為有彈性，所以可以彎曲而不會折斷。

Her *flexible* attitude helps her to deal with all kinds of people.
她柔順的態度，有助於應付各式各樣的人。

float 〔flot〕 *v.* 漂流

The raft will *float* down the river with the current. 這隻橡皮艇會在河中，順著水流的方向漂流。

flow 〔flo〕 *n.* 流

The *flow* of electricity was interrupted during the storm. 電流在暴風雨期間中斷了。

flu 〔flu〕 *n.* 流行性感冒

If you have the *flu*, you should **get a** lot of rest. 如果你感冒了，就應該要多休息。

fluctuate 〔'flʌktʃu,et〕 *v.* 波動

Vegetable prices *fluctuate* with the supply. 蔬菜的價格隨著供應量而波動。

fluent 〔'fluənt〕 *adj.* 流利的

He is a *fluent* speaker of French because he lived in France when **he** was a child. 他法文說得很流利，因爲他小時候住在法國。

focus 〔'fokəs〕 *v.* 對準焦點；集中（注意力）

The photograph is blurry because I didn't *focus* the camera correctly. 這張相片很模糊，因爲我沒有正確地將相機對準焦點。

I have to *focus* on studying math tonight because there will be **an exam** tomorrow. 我今晚必須集中注意力唸數學，因爲明天要考試。

fold〔 fold 〕*v.* 摺疊

Do not *fold* the paper, or you may damage the painting.

不要摺到紙，否則你可能會破壞這幅畫。

follow-on〔'falo'an〕*adj.* 後繼的

After he completes basic training, the private will begin his *follow-on* training in electronics.

當這名二等兵完成基礎訓練後，就要開始接受之後的電子學方面的訓練。

forbid〔 fə'bɪd 〕*v.* 禁止

The city government voted to *forbid* smoking in all public buildings.

市政府投票表決，禁止在公共建築物裡抽煙。

foreign〔'fɔrɪn〕*adj.* 外國的

We often go abroad because we enjoy visiting *foreign* countries.

我們常出國，因爲我們喜歡去外國遊覽。

forest〔'fɔrɪst〕*n.* 森林

The hillside is covered with a thick *forest* of pine trees.

這片山坡被茂密的松林所覆蓋。

formal〔'fɔrml̩〕*adj.* 正式的

Because the party was a *formal* occasion, everyone was dressed in his or her best clothes.

因爲這個宴會是正式的場合，所以每個人都穿上自己最好的衣服。

former (ˈfɔrmɚ) *pron.*
前者 *adj.* 以前的

Both of your suggestions are good, but I prefer the *former* to the latter. 你的兩個建議都不錯，但我喜歡前者甚於後者。

The *former* professor began a new career as a writer. 那位之前當過教授的人，現在開始改行當作家。

formula (ˈfɔrmjələ)
n. 公式

I did not do well on the chemistry test because I forgot an important *formula*. 我化學考試沒考好，因為我忘了一個重要的公式。

forward (ˈfɔrwəd)
adv. 向前

The sergeant gave the command for the soldiers to move *forward*. 這位中士命令士兵向前移動。

foundation
(faunˈdeʃən) *n.* 基礎

Because he had a good *foundation* in science, the student found the physics course relatively easy. 因為這名學生在科學方面的基礎很好，所以他覺得物理這門課相當簡單。

fracture (ˈfræktʃɚ)
n. 骨折

Although the car accident was bad, the driver only suffered a *fracture* in his arm. 雖然車禍很嚴重，但駕駛人只有手臂骨折。

frame 〔 frem 〕 *n.* 框架

The artist placed his new painting in a wooden *frame*.
畫家將他的新畫作裱在木框中。

frequency
〔 'frikwənsı 〕 *n.* 頻率

The *frequency* of traffic accidents has decreased thanks to the new traffic light.
多虧有新的交通號誌燈，使得發生交通意外事故的頻率減少。

fresh 〔 frɛʃ 〕 *adj.* 新鮮的

The salad was full of *fresh* vegetables.
這盤沙拉裝滿了新鮮的蔬菜。

friendly 〔 'frɛndlı 〕 *adj.*
友善的

His *friendly* expression made us feel welcome.
他友善的表情使我們感覺到受歡迎。

fuel 〔 'fjuəl 〕 *n.* 燃料

The car stopped when it ran out of *fuel*. 這輛車在燃料用完後，停了下來。

fume 〔 fjum 〕 *n.* 煙霧

Fumes from the engine filled the garage.
引擎冒出來的煙，充滿了整個車庫。

fundamental
〔 ˌfʌndə'mɛntḷ 〕 *adj.*
基本的

Addition and subtraction are *fundamental* concepts of mathematics.
加法和減法是數學中最基本的概念。

furnish 〔'fɝnɪʃ〕 *v.*
佈置；裝備傢俱

We will *furnish* the extra bedroom as soon as we have enough money.

等我們一有足夠的錢，就會佈置這間額外的臥房。

furnished 〔'fɝnɪʃt〕
adj. 附有傢俱的

He paid extra for a *furnished* apartment.

他付額外的錢，租了一間附傢俱的公寓。

furthermore
〔'fɝðɚ,mor〕 *adv.* 此外

We decided not to go on the picnic because it was too cold, and, *furthermore*, it looked like it was going to rain.

因為天氣太冷，所以我們決定不去野餐了，而且看起來好像快下雨了。

fuselage 〔'fjuzlɪdʒ〕
n. 機身

The wings of the airplane were damaged in the crash, but the *fuselage* was not.

飛機的機翼在墜毀時損壞了，但機身卻並未受損。

G

garbage 〔'gɑrbɪdʒ 〕
n. 垃圾

There was a lot of *garbage* in the park, such as newspapers and food wrappers. 公園裡有一大堆垃圾，像是報紙和食物的包裝紙。

gather 〔'gæðɚ 〕 *v.* 聚集

The neighbors often *gather* in the park in the evening.
鄰居們傍晚常聚集在公園裡。

gathering 〔'gæðɚɪŋ 〕
n. 聚會

The party was a friendly *gathering* of friends and relatives.
這個派對是朋友和親戚的愉快聚會。

general 〔'dʒɛnərəl 〕
adj. 概略的；普遍的

The photographer's lecture gave us a *general* idea of how to take better photographs.
這位攝影師的演講，告訴我們如何把相片拍得更好的概念。

After we lost the game, the *general* feeling was one of disappointment.
在我們輸了這場比賽之後，普遍的感覺都是失望。

generate 〔'dʒɛnə,ret 〕
v. 產生

A windmill is a traditional way to *generate* power.
風車是產生動力的傳統工具。

generator
(ˈdʒɛnəˌretə) *n.* 發電機

The *generator* produced electricity during the blackout.
發電機會在停電時產生電力。

generous (ˈdʒɛnərəs)
adj. 慷慨的

Our new neighbor is quite *generous*; he often donates money to charity.
我們的新鄰居相當慷慨；他常捐錢給慈善機構。

geography
(dʒiˈɑgrəfɪ) *n.* 地理學

The study of *geography* can teach us a lot about the earth.
研讀地理，可以讓我們知道很多有關地球的知識。

gift (gɪft) *n.* 禮物

The birthday *gift* was wrapped in colorful paper.
那個生日禮物被用鮮豔的包裝紙包著。

glance (glæns) *v.* , *n.*
瞥見；很快看一眼

He *glanced* at the headlines and then gave me the newspaper.
他將標題大略瀏覽一下，就把報紙給我。

glasses (glæsɪz) *n.pl.*
眼鏡

My grandmother needs to wear *glasses* when she reads.
我祖母看書時需要戴眼鏡。

glow (glo) *v.* 發光

My new watch will *glow* in the dark.
我的新手錶在黑暗中會發光。

glue 〔 glu 〕 *n.* 膠水
v. 黏

Use this *glue* to stick the picture on the card.
用這種膠水將圖畫貼在卡片上。

The cup is broken, but I think I can *glue* it back together.
杯子破掉了，但是我想我可以把它黏回去。

goggles 〔 'gɑglz 〕 *n.pl.*
護目鏡

It is one of the company rules that you must wear *goggles* while working. 工作時必須要戴護目鏡，是這家公司的規定之一。

goods 〔 gʊdz 〕 *n.pl.* 商品

The *goods* in this store are of good quality, but they are not expensive.
這家店的商品品質很好，但是不貴。

govern 〔 'gʌvən 〕 *v.*
統治；治理

In a monarchy, a king or queen *governs* the country.
在君主專制政體下，是由國王或女王治理國家。

government
〔 'gʌvənmənt 〕 *n.* 政府

An official from the *government* explained the new policy.
政府的一名官員出面說明這個新政策。

governor 〔 'gʌvənə 〕
n. 州長

This state will elect a new *governor* this year. 這個州今年將選出新的州長。

grade 〔gred〕*n.* 年級

The boys are the same age and they are in the same *grade* at school.

這些男孩的年紀相同,而且在學校裡就讀同一年級。

gradual〔'grædʒuəl〕
adj. 逐漸的

He made *gradual* progress in his studies.

他在學業上逐漸有進步。

gradually
〔'grædʒuəlɪ〕*adv.* 逐漸地

Losing weight *gradually* is much healthier than going on a strict diet.

逐漸的減重,比嚴厲的節食要健康多了。

grandchild
〔'græn,tʃaɪld〕*n.* 孫子;
孫女

Although the couple have four children, they have only one *grandchild*.

雖然這對夫婦有四個孩子,但卻只有一個孫子。

granddaughter
〔'græn,dɔtɚ〕*n.* 孫女

My *granddaughter* looks just like her mother did at that age.

我的孫女看起來就像她媽媽當年的樣子。

grandson〔'græn,sʌn〕
n. 孫子

My *grandson* will begin school next year.

我的孫子明年要開始去上學了。

graph〔græf〕*n.* 曲線圖；圖表

This *graph* shows the population growth over the last 20 years. 這張圖表顯示過去二十年的人口成長。

gravity〔'grævətɪ〕*n.* 地心引力；重力

In space the astronauts must cope with a lack of *gravity* and learn to control their movements as they float around. 在太空中，太空人必須要應付無重力狀態，而且要學習在四處漂浮時，控制自己的動作。

gray〔gre〕*adj.* 灰色的；灰白的

He is an old man with a *gray* beard. 他是一位留有灰白鬍子的老人。

graze〔grez〕*v.* 吃草

The farmer put the cows out to *graze* in the field. 農夫將乳牛群放到草原上吃草。

grind〔graɪnd〕*v.* 磨碎

The pepper mill will *grind* the peppercorns into powder. 胡椒磨碎機能將乾胡椒磨成粉末狀。

grip〔grɪp〕*v.* 緊抓

The carpenter *gripped* the saw with both hands. 木匠用雙手緊抓著鋸子。

gripe〔graɪp〕*v.* 抱怨；發牢騷

Don't *gripe* about the housework; we all have to lend a hand. 不要抱怨做家事；我們所有人都必須幫忙。

groove 〔gruv〕*n.* 細長
的凹槽；溝紋

There is a *groove* in the floor where
the door slides back and forth.
在門來回滑動的地板上，有個細長的凹槽。

group 〔grup〕*n.* 群；
團體

A *group* of five or six people was
waiting for the bus.
有一群約五個到六個人，正在等公車。

growth 〔groθ〕*n.* 成長

The government is predicting a high
rate of *growth* for the economy this
year.
政府預測，今年的經濟會有高成長率。

guard 〔gɑrd〕*v.* 看守

He is on duty at the gate; his job is
to *guard* it.
他在大門口值班；他的工作就是看守大門。

guest 〔gɛst〕*n.* 客人

I was a *guest* of the Smiths, and I
stayed in their home.
我是史密斯家的客人，而且我還住在他
們家。

guidance 〔'gaɪdəns〕
n. 指導；輔導

The counselor offered *guidance* to
the students as they were choosing
their courses.
輔導員指導學生如何選課。

guide 〔 gaɪd 〕 *v.* 引導

The man agreed to *guide* us around the city.

這名男子同意要帶我們四處參觀這個城市。

guilty 〔'gɪltɪ 〕 *adj.* 犯罪的；有罪的

The man insisted that he was not *guilty* of the crime; he swore that he hadn't done it.

這個男人堅持他沒有犯罪；他發誓說他沒有做這件事。

guitar 〔 gɪ'tɑr 〕 *n.* 吉他

Billy learned to play the *guitar* in music class.

比利在音樂課學彈吉他。

guy 〔 gaɪ 〕 *n.* 男人；傢伙

Everyone thinks that he is a good *guy* because he is always willing to help others.

每個人都覺得他是個好男人，因爲他總是樂於幫助別人。

【劉毅老師的話】

　　學說英語最快的方法，就是背「一口氣英語」，背了不會忘，背了一回就是一回，英文會說了，其他就簡單了。

H

habit 〔'hæbɪt 〕 *n.* 習慣

She has a *habit* of biting her pencil when she faces a difficult problem.
當她面臨困難的問題時，會習慣性地咬著鉛筆。

hammer 〔'hæmɚ 〕 *n.* 鐵鎚

If I had a *hammer*, I could nail these two boards together.
如果我有一把鐵鎚，我就可以把這兩塊木板釘在一起。

handicap 〔'hændɪ,kæp 〕 *n.* 不利的條件；障礙

Her inability to see well in the dark was a *handicap* when she had to drive a car at night.
當她必須在晚上開車時，無法在黑暗中看清楚，就是她的障礙。

handle 〔'hændl̩ 〕 *n.* 把手

Because the *handle* was broken, it was very difficult to carry the heavy suitcase.
因爲把手斷了，所以要提這個沉重的手提箱很困難。

handsome 〔'hænsəm 〕 *adj.* 英俊的

He looks very *handsome* in his new suit. 他穿新的西裝，看起來很英俊。

hardly (ˈhɑrdlɪ) *adv.*
幾乎不

With the exam approaching, I have *hardly* any free time.
隨著考試的接近,我幾乎沒有任何空閒時間。

hardship (ˈhɑrdʃɪp)
n. 艱難;辛苦

After their father lost his job, the children experienced *hardship*.
在他們的父親失業後,這些孩子歷盡艱辛。

hardworking
(ˈhɑrdˈwɝkɪŋ) *adj.* 辛勤工作的;努力的

The secretary is very *hardworking* and can always get the work done on time.
這位秘書非常辛勤工作,而且總是能夠準時完成工作。

harvest (ˈhɑrvɪst) *n.*
收穫;收成

Thanks to the good weather, the farmers had a good *harvest*.
由於天氣很好,使得農民們有好收成。

head (hɛd) *n.* 領導者
v. 領導;主持

He was the *head* of the country for nearly twenty years before he lost an election. 他在輸掉選戰之前,已擔任這個國家的領導人快二十年了。

Although she was busy, Mrs. Pearson agreed to *head* the fund-raising committee. 儘管皮爾森女士十分忙碌,她還是答應主持這個募款委員會。

health 〔 hɛlθ 〕 *n.* 健康

He is in very good *health* because he exercises regularly.
他的健康狀況十分良好，因爲他定期做運動。

heating 〔'hitɪŋ 〕 *n.* 暖氣

The new apartment has central *heating* and air conditioning.
這棟新公寓有中央暖氣和空調。

helmet 〔'hɛlmɪt 〕 *n.* 頭盔；安全帽

If you do not wear a *helmet* while riding a motorcycle, you may get a ticket. 如果你騎機車不戴安全帽，可能會被開罰單。

helpless 〔'hɛlplɪs 〕 *adj.* 無助的；不能自立的

The newborn baby was *helpless*; it could only cry when it wanted something. 新生兒是無法獨立的，當他們想要某種東西時，只會哭。

hesitate 〔'hɛzə,tet 〕 *v.* 猶豫

Unsure who could be calling him so late, John *hesitated* before answering the phone.
因爲不確定誰會這麼晚打電話給他，約翰在接電話之前猶豫了一下。

hinge 〔 hɪndʒ 〕 *n.* 鉸鏈

The door is not level because one of the *hinges* is broken.
門不太平穩，因爲其中一條鉸鏈斷了。

historic (hɪs'tɔrɪk)
adj. 具有歷史意義的

The end of World War II was a *historic* occasion. 第二次世界大戰的結束,是具有歷史意義的事件。

history ('hɪstrɪ) *n.* 歷史

The king was an important person in the *history* of the country. 這位國王在該國的歷史上,是一位重要的人物。

hoist (hɔɪst) *v.* 吊起
(重物)

The workers used a crane to *hoist* the materials to the roof of the building. 工人們用起重機,將材料吊到樓頂。

hole (hol) *n.* 洞

This sock has a *hole* in it. Can you fix it? 這隻襪子破了一個洞。你可以修補嗎?

holiday ('halə,de) *n.*
假日

Independence Day is a national *holiday*. 獨立紀念日是國定假日。

honest ('anɪst) *adj.*
誠實的;正直的

He is an *honest* man; he could not have stolen the money. 他是個正直的人;不可能會偷錢。

honeymoon
('hʌnɪ,mun) *n.* 蜜月

The newlyweds went to Italy for their *honeymoon*. 這對新婚夫婦去義大利渡蜜月。

honorable (ˈɑnərəbḷ)
adj. 光榮的；表揚榮譽的

When he retired, the colonel was given an *honorable* discharge.

當這位上校退休時，他被頒發榮譽解職證。

horizon (həˈraɪzṇ)
n. 地平線

At the end of the day everyone gathered to watch the sun sink below the *horizon*.

在一天快結束時，每個人都聚集來看太陽落到地平線以下。

host (host) *n.* 主人

He is a wonderful *host* and always throws a good party.

他是一位很棒的主人，總是舉辦很好的派對。

hover (ˈhʌvɚ) *v.* 盤旋

The pilot of the helicopter was able to *hover* over the site of the accident.

這架直升機的駕駛員，能在意外發生的地點上空盤旋。

huge (hjudʒ) *adj.* 巨大的

The elephant is a *huge* animal when compared with the mouse.

和老鼠比起來，大象算是十分巨大的動物。

hull (hʌl) *n.* 船身

The *hull* of the Titanic was damaged by an iceberg.

鐵達尼號的船身被冰山撞毀。

human (ˈhjumən) *n.* 人

The chimpanzee is a very intelligent animal; it can copy the behavior of *humans*. 黑猩猩是非常聰明的動物；牠們會模仿人類的行為舉止。

humor (ˈhjumɚ) *n.* 幽默

His sense of *humor* is a little strange; not everyone understands his jokes. 他的幽默感有點奇怪；不是每個人都能了解他的笑話。

humorous (ˈhjumərəs) *adj.* 幽默的；好笑的

The film was advertised as a comedy, but I did not find it *humorous* at all. 這部影片被宣傳為喜劇片，但我覺得它一點都不好笑。

hydrogen (ˈhaɪdrədʒən) *n.* 氫

We must be careful with the *hydrogen* because it is an explosive gas. 我們必須小心處理氫氣，因為它是易爆炸的氣體。

```
hydro  +  gen
  |         |
water  +  produce
```

hypothesis (haɪˈpɑθəsɪs) *n.* 假設

He presented his *hypothesis* after careful study. 在仔細地研究之後，他提出了他的假設。

I

ideal ﹝ aɪ'diəl ﹞ *adj.*
理想的；完美的

The weather is *ideal* for a picnic today; it's warm and sunny.
今天的天氣適合野餐；旣溫暖又晴朗。

identify ﹝ aɪ'dɛntə‚faɪ ﹞
v. 辨識；認出

The victim was unable to *identify* the thief because he had worn a mask.
受害者無法認出小偷是誰，因爲他戴了面具。

ignore ﹝ ɪg'nor ﹞ *v.* 忽視

Don't *ignore* the pain in your shoulder. You should see a doctor and make sure that it is nothing serious.
不要忽視你肩膀上的疼痛。你應該去看醫生，以確定它並不嚴重。

illegal ﹝ ɪ'ligl ﹞ *adj.*
違法的

It is *illegal* for you to smoke if you are under 18.
如果你未滿十八歲就吸煙，是違法的。

image ﹝ 'ɪmɪdʒ ﹞ *n.*
影像；形象

We called a repairman because the *image* on the TV screen was fuzzy.
我們叫了修理工來，因爲電視螢幕上的影像模糊不清。

imitate ﹝ 'ɪmə‚tet ﹞ *v.*
模仿

It is difficult to *imitate* his handwriting.　他的筆跡很難模仿。

immediate〔ɪ'midɪɪt〕
adj. 立刻的

As soon as we heard about the approaching typhoon, we took *immediate* steps to protect our home. 當我們一聽說颱風接近的消息,就立即採取保護家園的措施。

impact〔'ɪmpækt〕*n.*
撞擊力;影響

He fell from the tree, and when he hit the ground, the *impact* broke his arm. 他從樹上掉下來,當他撞到地面時的衝擊力,使他的手臂折斷了。

implement
〔'ɪmpləmənt〕*v.* 實施

We will *implement* the new policy at the beginning of next year. 我們將在明年初實施這項新政策。

im + ple + ment
| | |
in + *fill* + *n.*

imply〔ɪm'plaɪ〕*v.* 暗示

Although she scolded the children, her smile *implied* that she was not really angry. 雖然她責罵這些小孩,但她的笑容卻暗示,她並非真的在生氣。

import〔ɪm'port〕*v.*
進口;輸入

Because it produces no oil of its own, the country must *import* it. 因為該國沒有出產石油,所以必須進口石油。

im + port
| |
in + *carry*

impossible
〔 ɪm'pɑsəbḷ 〕 *adj.*
不可能的

It's *impossible* to get an appointment with the dentist this week unless it is an emergency; he is fully booked.

這星期除非是急診，否則不可能跟這位牙醫師約時間；因爲他的時間已經全排滿了。

impression
〔 ɪm'prɛʃən 〕 *n.* 印象

The effective way the mayor handled the problem made a good *impression* on everyone.

這位市長以有效的方式處理問題，給每個人留下很好的印象。

improve〔 ɪm'pruv 〕
v. 改善

If you study harder, you will be able to *improve* your grades.

如果你更用功唸書，就能使你的成績進步。

incapable〔 ɪn'kepəbḷ 〕
adj. 不能的

I am *incapable* of repairing my own car, so I take it to a mechanic.

我不會修理我自己的車，所以我把它交給機械工修理。

include〔 ɪn'klud 〕*v.*
包括

The apartment is 30,000 dollars per month, *including* gas and electricity.

這間公寓每個月要三萬元，含瓦斯和電。

```
in + clude
 |      |
in  +  shut
```

income (ˈɪn͵kʌm) *n.* 收入

Alice's mother enjoys her work as a nurse, but she does not have an *income*. 愛麗絲的媽媽喜歡護士這份工作，但是她沒有收入。

incomplete (͵ɪnkəmˈplit) *adj.* 不完整的

The set of encyclopedia is *incomplete*; we are missing the last three volumes. 這套百科全書並不完整；我們缺了最後三冊。

incorporate (ɪnˈkɔrpə͵ret) *v.* 將～併入；將～編入

The advanced course will *incorporate* more challenging projects. 高級課程會編入更多具有挑戰性的計劃。

indicate (ˈɪndə͵ket) *v.* 指出；表示

The bike rider *indicated* that he was going to turn by holding out his arm. 腳踏車騎士表示，他轉彎時會放開一隻手臂。

individual (͵ɪndəˈvɪdʒʊəl) *n.* 個人；人

The principal gave every *individual* involved in the prank the same punishment. 校長給每個涉入這場惡作劇的人同樣的處罰。

industrial (ɪnˈdʌstrɪəl) *adj.* 工業的

It is unlikely that anyone would want to build a house in the *industrial* area of town. 不可能有人會想把房子建在城裡的工業區。

industry〔'ɪndəstrɪ〕
n. 產業；工業

Electronics is an important *industry* in this state.
電子業是這一州的重要產業。

infect〔ɪn'fɛkt〕*v.* 傳染

Cover your mouth when you cough so that you don't *infect* anyone else.
當你咳嗽時，請摀住嘴巴，
以免傳染給其他人。

```
in + fect
|      |
in + put
```

inferior〔ɪn'fɪrɪɚ〕
adj. 比～差的；下級的

The rank of lieutenant is *inferior* to that of colonel.
中尉的官階比上校低。

infantry〔'ɪnfəntrɪ〕
n. 步兵團

Soldiers in the *infantry* must do a lot of walking.
步兵團的士兵必須走很多路。

inflexible
〔ɪn'flɛksəbl̩〕*adj.* 不易彎
曲的；強硬的

This metal is *inflexible*; you cannot bend it unless you heat it.
這種金屬是不易彎曲的；除非你將它加熱，
否則無法使它彎曲。

```
in + flex + ible
|      |      |
not + bend + adj.
```

My parents are so *inflexible*; I can never change their minds.
我的父母非常強硬；我絕對無法改變他們
的想法。

influence (ˈɪnfluəns)
v.,n. 影響

The weather may ***influence*** our plans for the weekend.
天氣可能會影響我們週末的計劃。

inform (ɪnˈfɔrm) *v.*
通知

The pilot ***informed*** the passengers that they were approaching the airport.
飛行員通知乘客，他們即將抵達機場。

informal (ɪnˈfɔrml̩)
adj. 非正式的

The party is ***informal*** so there is no need to get all dressed up.
這是非正式的宴會，所以不需要盛裝打扮。

inhale (ɪnˈhel) *v.* 吸氣

The doctor asked me to ***inhale*** deeply while he listened to my lungs.
當醫生聽我的肺時，他要求我深吸一口氣。

```
in +  hale
 |      |
in + breathe
```

initial (ɪˈnɪʃəl) *adj.*
最初的

His ***initial*** reaction to our plan was negative, but we eventually persuaded him to agree. 他對我們的計劃的最初反應是否定的，但我們最後說服他同意了。

inject (ɪnˈdʒɛkt) *v.*
注射

The nurse will ***inject*** the vaccine into your arm. 護士會在你的手臂注射疫苗。

```
in +  ject
 |      |
in + throw
```

injure 〔ˈɪndʒɚ〕 *v.*
使受傷

She *injured* her leg when she fell
down the stairs.

當她從樓梯上摔下來時，傷到了腿。

injury 〔ˈɪndʒərɪ〕 *n.* 傷

Steve cut his finger, but the *injury* is
not serious.

史帝夫切到手指，但傷勢並不嚴重。

in-law 〔ˈɪnˌlɔ〕 *n.* 姻親

We had dinner with my *in-laws*
because my wife wanted to discuss
something with her parents.

我和我的姻親一起吃晚餐，因為我太太想
要和她的父母討論一些事情。

inner 〔ˈɪnɚ〕 *adj.* 內部的

There is something wrong with the
inner part of the weapon.

這件武器的內部有點問題。

innocent 〔ˈɪnəsn̩t〕
adj. 清白的

When the trial began, the defendant
declared that he was *innocent*.

當審判開始時，該名被告宣稱他是清白的。

input 〔ˈɪnˌpʊt〕 *n.*
投入；輸入

I hope you will all attend the meeting
because we need everyone's *input* in
order to find a solution to the problem.

我希望你們全都可以參加這場會議，因為
我們需要每個人都投入，為這個問題找出
解決辦法。

inquire〔 ɪn'kwaɪr 〕
v. 詢問

I went to the information counter to *inquire* about the bus schedule.

我到服務台詢問公車
時刻表。

```
in + quire
 |     |
in + search
```

insect〔'ɪnsɛkt 〕 *n.* 昆蟲

The butterfly is a flying *insect*.
蝴蝶是會飛的昆蟲。

insignia〔 ɪn'sɪgnɪə 〕
n. 徽章；勳章

The *insignia* on a soldier's uniform indicates his rank.

士兵制服上的徽章能
顯示他的階級。

```
in + sign + ia
 |     |     |
on + mark + n.
```

insist〔 ɪn'sɪst 〕 *v.* 堅持

Despite the evidence against him, he *insisted* that he was innocent.
儘管證據對他不利，他還是堅持自己是清白的。

I *insist* on paying for the damage; after all, the accident was my fault.
我堅持要賠償損害；畢竟，這場意外是我的錯。

inspect〔 ɪn'spɛkt 〕 *v.*
檢查

I will *inspect* your work when you are finished. 在你完成工作後，我會來檢查。

```
in  + spect
 |     |
into +  see (窺視內部)
```

install ﹝ ɪn'stɔl ﹞ *v.*
安裝

The car dealer promised to *install* a new battery in the car.
車商承諾要替車子裝上新電池。

installation
﹝ˌɪnstə'leʃən﹞ *n.* 安裝

We had a mechanic help us with the *installation* of the car battery.
我們請一位技工協助我們安裝汽車的電池。

instant ﹝'ɪnstənt﹞ *n.*
瞬間；片刻

I closed the door and, in an *instant,* realized that I had locked myself out.
在關上門時，我立刻就知道，我把自己鎖在門外了。

instantaneous
﹝ˌɪnstən'tenɪəs﹞ *adj.*
立即的；瞬間的

The effect of the medicine was *instantaneous*; I felt better immediately.
這個藥的藥效是立即性的；我馬上覺得好多了。

instruct ﹝ ɪn'strʌkt ﹞
v. 教導

The sergeant will *instruct* you in the proper way to clean your weapon.
中士將教導你，如何適當地清理武器。

instrument
﹝'ɪnstrəmənt﹞ *n.* 器具；
樂器

Of all the musical *instruments,* I like the piano best.
在所有的樂器當中，我最喜歡鋼琴。

insulate (ˈɪnsəˌlet)
v. 使隔離

It is important to *insulate* yourself from live electricity in order to avoid a shock.

為了避免觸電，使自己和通電的電流隔離是很重要的。

insulated (ˈɪnsəˌletɪd)
adj. 與外界絕緣的

All of the electrical wires in the house are *insulated* to make them safer to handle.

房子裡的所有電線都與外界絕緣，這樣觸摸到時，才會比較安全。

insulation
(ˌɪnsəˈleʃən) *n.* 絕緣體

Insulation protects electricians from shocks when they are handling wires.

絕緣體保護電工，讓他們在觸摸電線時不會觸電。

insulator (ˌɪnsəˈletɚ)
n. 絕緣體

Rubber is a widely used *insulator*.

橡皮是被人們廣泛使用的絕緣體。

integrity (ɪnˈtɛgrətɪ)
n. 正直

It is important to have *integrity* or soon no one will believe you.

正直是很重要的，否則很快地就沒有人會相信你了。

intelligent
(ɪnˈtɛlədʒənt) *adj.*
聰明的

The boy is very *intelligent*; he began to read at the age of three.

這個男孩非常聰明；他從三歲就開始閱讀。

intense 〔 ɪn'tɛns 〕 *adj.*
密集的

The new recruits had to undergo *intense* training.
新兵必須接受密集的訓練。

intention 〔 ɪn'tɛnʃən 〕
n. 企圖

It is the professor's *intention* to cover all the material in the book by the end of the semester.
教授企圖在學期末之前，將這本書的所有資料都教完。

interest 〔'ɪntrɪst 〕 *v.*
使感興趣

This movie does not *interest* me at all.
這部電影一點都無法引起我的興趣。

interfere 〔,ɪntɚ'fɪr 〕
v. 妨礙

The music *interfered* with my concentration when I was trying to study. 在我想要唸書時，音樂妨礙我集中注意力。

```
 inter  +  fere
   |         |
between + strike
```

intermediate
〔,ɪntɚ'midɪɪt 〕 *adj.* 中級的

If you pass this exam, you will be able to move on to the *intermediate* course.
如果你通過這次考試，你將可以進階到中級的課程。

international

(ˌɪntəˈnæʃənḷ) *adj.*
國際的

The flight between New York and London is an ***international*** trip.
在紐約和倫敦之間的航程是國際的旅程。

```
inter  + national
  |         |
between + national
```

interpret (ɪnˈtɝprɪt)

v. 解釋；口譯

The doctor was able to ***interpret*** the test results for me.
醫生可以將檢驗的結果解釋給我聽。

The tour guide will ***interpret*** for the visitors when they go to the market.
當旅客到市場時，導遊會爲他們進行口譯。

interrupt (ˌɪntəˈrʌpt)

v. 打斷；使中斷

The TV program was ***interrupted*** by a public announcement.
電視節目因發佈一項公告而中斷了。

```
inter  + rupt
  |        |
between + break
```

intersect (ˌɪntəˈsɛkt)

v. 相交

Place the sign where the two roads ***intersect***.
將告示放在兩條路相交的地方。

```
inter  + sect
  |        |
between + cut
```

interval 〔'ɪntɚvl̩ 〕 *n.*
（時間的）間隔

In this company the employees are evaluated at six month *intervals*.
在這家公司，每隔六個月，就會評鑑員工一次。

intestinal 〔 ɪn'tɛstɪnl̩ 〕
adj. 腸的

There was an outbreak of *intestinal* flu and many people called in sick.
腸胃型流行性感冒爆發，許多人都打電話來請病假。

intestine 〔 ɪn'tɛstɪn 〕
n. 腸

The large *intestine* is an important part of the digestive system.
大腸是消化系統中的重要部位。

invent 〔 ɪn'vɛnt 〕 *v.*
發明

The scientist hopes to *invent* a device that will improve the way we communicate. 那位科學家希望能發明一種裝置，改善我們的溝通方式。

inventory 〔'ɪnvə,torɪ 〕
n. 存貨清單

The clerk checked the *inventory* to see if the product was in stock.
店員檢查了存貨清單，看這項產品是否還有庫存。

investigate
〔 ɪn'vɛstə,get 〕 *v.* 調查

Whenever a plane crashes, an official will *investigate* the cause of the crash.
每當有飛機墜毀，就會有官員調查失事原因。

```
in + vestigate
|       |
in +    trace
```

invitation

(͵ɪnvə'teʃən) *n.*

請帖；邀請

According to the ***invitation***, the party will begin at 7:30.

根據這張請帖，宴會將在七點半開始。

involve (ɪn'valv) *v.*

牽涉；捲入

If you get ***involved*** in that project, you will be very busy.

如果你參與那個計劃，你將會變得很忙碌。

```
in + volve
  |      |
in +  roll
```

iron ('aɪən) *n.* 鐵

Iron is a very strong metal, but it rusts easily.

鐵是很堅固的金屬，但是它很容易生銹。

irresponsible

(͵ɪrɪ'spansəbḷ) *adj.*

不負責任的

He is very ***irresponsible*** so don't trust him with anything important.

他很不負責任，所以不要委託他任何重要的事。

irritate ('ɪrə͵tet) *v.*

激怒；刺激

People who talk loudly in the library ***irritate*** me.

在圖書館大聲說話的人，會激怒我。

I am allergic to this soap; it ***irritates*** my skin.

我對這塊肥皂過敏；它會刺激我的皮膚。

island (ˈaɪlənd) *n.* 島

The *island* is connected to the mainland by a bridge.

這座島是以一座橋和大陸連接。

isolate (ˈaɪsḷˌet) *v.* 使隔離

We must *isolate* the sick people so that the disease does not spread.

我們必須隔離這些病人，這樣疾病才不會蔓延。

issue (ˈɪʃu,ˈɪʃju) *v.* 發給；配給

During the orientation, every soldier was *issued* a uniform and other equipment.

在新兵訓練期間，都會發給每位士兵一件制服和其他裝備。

【劉毅老師的話】

　　23813148 這個數字不好背，如果改成：2-381-3148 就容易多了。背單字也是一樣，一定要分音節來背，才不會忘記。

J

jog〔dʒɑg〕*v.* 慢跑

As part of his fitness program, he *jogs* every morning.
每天早上慢跑，是他健身計劃中的一部份。

join〔dʒɔɪn〕*v.* 參加

She has decided to *join* the air force after graduation.
她已經決定，畢業後要加入空軍。

judge〔dʒʌdʒ〕*n.* 法官
v. 判斷；擔任評審

A *judge* must be fair and impartial.
法官必須公正而且公平。

It is not always wise to *judge* people by their appearance.
以貌取人未必是明智的。

Professor Brown agreed to *judge* the speech competition.
布朗教授同意要擔任演講比賽的評審。

judgment
〔'dʒʌdʒmənt〕*n.* 判斷

In her *judgment*, he is a careless and irresponsible person.
依她的判斷，他是一個粗心而且不負責任的人。

judicial〔dʒu'dɪʃəl〕
adj. 司法的

The United States' *judicial* system includes both state and federal courts.
美國的司法體系包含州法院和聯邦法院。

junk 〔 dʒʌŋk 〕*n.* 垃圾

There is a lot of *junk* in the yard; we should get rid of it.

院子裡有很多垃圾；我們應該清除它。

jury 〔 'dʒʊrɪ 〕*n.* 陪審團

After hearing all the evidence, the *jury* found the man guilty of the crime.

在聽完所有的證詞之後，陪審團判定這個男人有罪。

justice 〔 'dʒʌstɪs 〕*n.* 正義；公理

People expect to find *justice* in a court of law.

人們希望能在法院伸張正義。

【劉毅老師的話】

　　英文學好了，退伍以後，歡迎來找我，加入「劉毅英文」的教學團隊。什麼叫英文學好？只要能將「一口氣英語」背完，你的英文就等於學好了。

K

ketchup (ˈkɛtʃəp) *n.*
蕃茄醬

Would you like some *ketchup* or mustard on your hamburger?

你的漢堡要加一些蕃茄醬還是芥末？

keyboard (ˈkiˌbord)
n. 鍵盤

Use the computer *keyboard* to type your password.

用電腦鍵盤打出你的密碼。

kidney (ˈkɪdnɪ) *n.* 腎臟

Because both of her son's *kidneys* were damaged, she donated one of her kidneys to him.

因為他兒子的兩顆腎臟都壞了，所以她捐了一個腎臟給他。

kit (kɪt) *n.* 一組工具；
工具箱

You can find a bandage in the first aid *kit*.

你可以在急救箱裡找到繃帶。

knowledge (ˈnɑlɪdʒ)
n. 知識

You should talk to John about your investment; he has a lot of *knowledge* about finance.

你應該跟約翰說有關你的投資的事；他對於理財有豐富的知識。

L

lab 〔læb〕 *adj.* 實驗室的
n. 實驗室

After examining the *lab* results, the doctor wrote a prescription for the patient. 在仔細研究過實驗結果後,醫生開了一張處方給這位病人。

laboratory
〔'læbrə,torɪ〕 *n.* 實驗室
(= *lab*)

Dr. Miller sent a sample of the patient's blood to the *laboratory*. 米勒醫生送了一位病人的血液樣本到實驗室。

```
labora + tory
   |       |
 work  + place
```

lack 〔læk〕 *n., v.* 缺乏

After studying all night, he suffered from the *lack* of sleep. 在唸了整晚的書後,他感到睡眠不足。

Born poor, he *lacked* money all his life. 他出身窮困,一輩子都缺錢。

landmark
〔'lænd,mɑrk〕 *n.* 地標

The bridge is a good *landmark* that tells sailors they are near the harbor. 這座橋是一個很好的地標,它告訴船員們港口快到了。

lap 〔 læp 〕 *n.* 一圈；
一次往返

The swimming coach asked us to swim a couple of *laps* to warm up.
游泳教練要求我們，先游幾圈暖身。

latitude 〔 ˈlætəˌtjud 〕
n. 緯度
(*cf.* longitude *n.* 經度)

The equator is located at zero degrees *latitude*.
赤道是位於緯度零度的地方。

latter 〔 ˈlætɚ 〕 *pron.*
後者

I like both chocolate and strawberry ice cream, but if I have to choose, I'll take the *latter*.
巧克力和草莓冰淇淋我都喜歡，但是如果我必須作選擇，我會選後者。

launch 〔 lɔntʃ 〕 *v.*
開始；發動

The library will *launch* a new education program this month.
圖書館在本月將開辦新的教育課程。

lawyer 〔 ˈlɔjɚ 〕 *n.* 律師

The defendant could not afford a *lawyer*, so the court appointed one to defend him.
被告付不起錢請律師，所以法院就指派一位律師為他辯護。

layer 〔 ˈleɚ 〕 *n.* 一層

It is a good idea to put on another *layer* of clothes when the weather is cold. 天氣很冷時，再加穿一層衣物是個好主意。

lean 〔lin〕*v.* 傾身;斜倚

The sign says not to *lean* over the side of the bridge.

這個告示說,不要靠在橋邊。

Don't *lean* against that wall! It's just been painted.

不要靠在那面牆上!那才剛剛油漆過。

lease 〔lis〕*n.* 租賃契約

The couple signed only a six-month *lease* on the apartment because they plan to buy a house soon.

這對夫婦只簽訂了六個月的公寓租約,因為他們計劃不久之後要買房子。

lecture 〔'lɛktʃɚ〕*n.* 講課;演講

When Professor Cooper gives a *lecture*, he often uses a microphone so that everyone can hear him.

當庫培教授講課時,他常會使用麥克風,讓每個人都可以聽見他說的話。

legal 〔'ligḷ〕*adj.* 法定的;合法的

What is the *legal* drinking age in your country?

在你們國家,可以喝酒的法定年齡是幾歲?

legislature 〔'lɛdʒɪs,letʃɚ〕*n.* 立法院

The *legislature* passed a new law yesterday.

立法院昨天通過了一個新法案。

leisure (ˈliʒɚ) *adj.*
空閒的

Many people like to watch TV in their *leisure* time.
許多人喜歡在空閒時間看電視。

lenient (ˈlinɪənt) *adj.*
寬鬆的；仁慈的

The admission requirements of the school are very *lenient*; it is not difficult to get in.
這所學校的入學條件很寬鬆；要進入這所學校並不困難。

Because it was the criminal's first offense, the judge was *lenient* and gave him a light sentence.
因為這個犯人是初次犯罪，所以法官很仁慈地判他輕刑。

lens (lɛnz) *n.* 鏡片

Sunglasses are glasses with dark *lenses*. 太陽眼鏡是鑲深色鏡片的眼鏡。

level (ˈlɛvḷ) *adj.* 平坦的
n. 水準

The books fell off the shelf because it was not *level*. 因為書架不平穩，所以書就從上面掉了下來。

He has a high *level* of education.
他的教育水準很高。

lie (laɪ) *v.* 躺

Sue went to her room to *lie* down because she has a headache.
蘇走到她的房間躺下，因為她頭痛。

lieutenant〔luˈtɛnənt〕
n.（海軍）上尉

My father was a *lieutenant* in the
navy. 我父親是海軍上尉。

likewise〔ˈlaɪkˌwaɪz〕
adv. 同樣地；也

George believes it will rain today and
I think *likewise*, so let's cancel the
picnic. 喬治認為今天會下雨，而我也這
麼認為，所以我們取消野餐吧。

limit〔ˈlɪmɪt〕*v.* 限制
n. 極限

The doctor told me that in order to
lose weight I had to exercise and
limit the amount of calories I ate.
醫生告訴我，為了減重，我必須運動，而
且要限制我所吃進去的卡路里。

Two cups of coffee a day is my *limit*;
I can't drink any more. 一天喝兩杯咖
啡是我的極限了；我不能再多喝。

limited〔ˈlɪmɪtɪd〕
adj. 有限的

I have a *limited* amount of money to
spend, so I hope to find an inexpensive
gift for my sister.
我可以用的金額有限，所以我希望找到
一個不貴的禮物送我姊姊。

liquefy〔ˈlɪkwəˌfaɪ〕
v. 使熔化；使液化

Metal can be *liquefied* when it is
exposed to high heat.
金屬在接觸到高熱時會被熔化。

locate (lo'ket) *v.*
找出…的位置

I cannot **locate** Elm Street on this map.
我在這張地圖上找不到愛爾姆街的位置。

location (lo'keʃən)
n. 位置；地點

This is a good **location** for our picnic because the ground is dry and the trees provide some shade.
這是一個讓我們野餐的好位置，因為地面是乾的，而且有樹木遮蔭。

longitude
('lɑndʒə,tjud) *n.* 經度
(*cf.* latitude *n.* 緯度)

Longitude is a measurement that will tell you how far east or west you are of Greenwich, England.
經度是一種度量法，它可以指出你距離英國格林威治以東或以西多遠。

lottery ('lɑtərɪ) *n.* 彩券

I bought five **lottery** tickets in the hope of becoming a millionaire. 我買了五張樂透彩券，希望能變成百萬富翁。

loyal ('lɔɪəl) *adj.* 忠實的

I know I can trust you with a secret because you are such a **loyal** friend.
我知道我可以將祕密託付給你，因為你是個很忠實的朋友。

loyalty ('lɔɪəltɪ) *n.* 忠誠

The soldiers have a great sense of **loyalty** to their captain and always stand by him. 士兵們對他們的上尉非常忠誠，總是會支持他。

luck 〔 lʌk 〕 *n.* 幸運

I'm in *luck*. There is one space left on the European tour.

我很幸運。到歐洲旅遊的名額剛好剩下一位。

lucky 〔 'lʌkɪ 〕 *adj.* 幸運的

You were very *lucky* not to be hurt in that accident.

你很幸運，沒在那次的意外中受傷。

luncheon 〔 'lʌntʃən 〕 *n.* 午餐

Mrs. Adams had a *luncheon* to welcome her new neighbors.

亞當斯太太準備了午餐，要歡迎她的新鄰居。

lung 〔 lʌŋ 〕 *n.* 肺

When you inhale, your *lungs* fill with air.

當你吸氣時，你的肺就會充滿空氣。

luxury 〔 'lʌkʃərɪ 〕 *n.* 奢侈品

Diamonds are a *luxury* for most people.

對大多數的人而言，鑽石是奢侈品。

M

magazine 〔͵mægə'zin 〕
n. 彈匣;雜誌

There is one cartridge left in the *magazine*, so the weapon is still loaded. 彈匣中還剩一顆子彈,所以這件武器還是裝有子彈的。

magnet 〔'mægnɪt 〕 *n.*
磁鐵

Mr. Miller used a *magnet* to hold the paper on the refrigerator.
米勒先生用一塊磁鐵,讓那張紙吸附在冰箱上。

magnetic 〔 mæg'nɛtɪk 〕
adj. 有磁性的

A *magnetic* compass will show which direction is north.
有磁性的指南針,會顯示哪個方向是北方。

major 〔'medʒɚ 〕 *adj.*
主要的

Poor visibility was the *major* cause of the accident.
能見度低是發生這次意外的主因。

make 〔 mek 〕 *v.* 使

Flowers will *make* the room look more cheerful.
花朵會使這個房間,看起來更明亮而舒適。

male 〔 mel 〕 *n.* 男性

Most of the new recruits are *male*.
大多數的新進人員都是男性。

mandatory
('mændə,torɪ) *adj.* 強制
的；義務性的

Your teacher says that participation in the activity is *mandatory*.
你們老師說，參與這項活動是強制性的。

maneuver (mə'nuvə)
n. 軍事演習 *v.* 移動

The *maneuvers* are designed to train the troops for combat.
軍事演習的目的，是為了要訓練部隊的戰鬥能力。

It will be difficult to *maneuver* this piano up the stairs.
要把這台鋼琴移上樓，是很困難的。

manner ('mænə) *n.*
方式；態度

His sales *manner* was so aggressive that it made me distrust him.
他的銷售方式太積極，使我不信任他。

manufacture
(,mænjə'fæktʃə) *v.* 製造

This product was *manufactured* in the United States.
這項產品是在美國製造的。

march (martʃ) *v.* 行軍

The sergeant ordered his men to *march* back to camp.
中士命令他的士兵們，行軍回到營地。

mark (mark) *n.* 痕跡

The spilled ink left a *mark* on the table. 灑出的墨水在桌子上留下了一個痕跡。

marksman

('mɑrksmən) *n.* 射擊
高手；狙擊手

He rarely misses the target because
he is a great *marksman*.
因為他是個神射手，所以很少打不中目標。

marksmanship

('mɑrksmən‚ʃɪp) *n.*
射擊術；箭術

He practiced his *marksmanship* on
the shooting range.
他在靶場練習射擊。

mask (mæsk) *n.* 面具

Because the thief was wearing a
mask, we have no idea what he looks
like. 因為小偷戴著面具，所以我們不知
道他長什麼樣子。

mass (mæs) *n.* 塊；團

An island is a *mass* of land surrounded
by water.
島嶼是一塊被水環繞的土地。

matter ('mætɚ) *n.* 物質

The scientists will analyze the object
to find out what kind of *matter* it is
composed of.
科學家們將分析這個物體，查出它是由哪
一種物質所組成的。

maximum

('mæksəməm) *adj.*
最大的

At this school the *maximum* class
size is twenty.
在這所學校，規模最大的班級是二十名
學生。

mayonnaise
〔͵meə′nez〕*n.* 美乃滋

The potato salad contains *mayonnaise*.
馬鈴薯沙拉有加美乃滋。

mean〔min〕*adj.*
惡劣的;卑鄙的

It was *mean* of you to criticize her
dress. 你批評她的服裝是很惡劣的。

means〔minz〕*n.* 方法

He accomplished the job, but the
means he used were unusual.
他完成了工作,但他用的方法很不尋常。

meanwhile
〔′min͵hwaɪl〕*adv.* 在這
期間;同時

You go to the post office; *meanwhile*,
I'll go to the market.
在你到郵局的期間,我會去市場。

mechanical
〔mə′kænɪkl̩〕*adj.* 機械
操作的

In order to repair a car, you must
have good *mechanical* ability.
要修理一台車,你必須要有良好的機械操
作能力。

mechanism
〔′mɛkə͵nɪzəm〕*n.*
機械裝置

The antique clock is composed of
many small *mechanisms*.
這個古董鐘是由許多微小的機械裝置所
組成。

medication
〔͵mɛdɪ′keʃən〕*n.* 藥物

The doctor said that this *medication*
should relieve my cough.
醫生說,這種藥應該可以減輕我的咳嗽。

melt 〔 mɛlt 〕 *v.* 融化

If you don't put the ice cream in the freezer, it will ***melt***.

如果你不把冰淇淋放到冰箱裡，它將會融化。

mental 〔 'mɛntḷ 〕 *adj.*
智能的；心理的

He has very good ***mental*** abilities, so it is no surprise that he gets good grades in school.

他的智力很高，所以在學校能拿高分，一點都不令人驚訝。

mention 〔 'mɛnʃən 〕
v. 提到

Bob didn't ***mention*** the accident when I saw him.

當我看到鮑伯時，他並沒有提到這場意外。

merchandise
〔 'mɜtʃən͵daɪz 〕 *n.* 商品

A discount store sells lower priced ***merchandise*** than a department store.

廉價商店賣的商品，價格比百貨公司低。

messy 〔 'mɛsɪ 〕 *adj.*
凌亂的

Your desk is so ***messy***! Why can't you be neater?

你的書桌太亂了！你為什麼不能整齊一點？

method 〔 'mɛθəd 〕 *n.*
方法

The chef was not familiar with the cooking ***method*** the recipe called for.

主廚不熟悉食譜上所需要的烹調方式。

microscope
〔'maɪkrəˌskop〕*n.* 顯微鏡

A *microscope* is standard equipment in a science laboratory.
顯微鏡是科學實驗室的標準配備。

```
micro + scope
  |       |
small  + look
```

middle〔'mɪdl̩〕*adj.*
中間的   *n.* 中間

Let's try to finish the project by the *middle* of the month.
我們試著在月中，就將這個計劃完成吧。

mild〔maɪld〕*adj.*
溫和的

Tom likes spring because the weather is *mild*.
湯姆喜歡春天，因為天氣很溫和。

mine〔maɪn〕*v.* 開採
n. 礦場

According to the geologist's report, this is a good place to *mine* for copper. 根據地質學家的報告，這裡是開採銅礦的好地點。

Working in a *mine* is a difficult job.
在礦場工作是很困難的。

mineral〔'mɪnərəl〕
n. 礦物

Diamonds are one of the most valuable *minerals*.
鑽石是最珍貴的礦物之一。

minimize ﹝'mɪnəˌmaɪz﹞
v. 把…減至最小；把…說
成極不重要

You can *minimize* your chance of
catching a cold by staying away from
crowded places.
遠離擁擠的地方，可以將你罹患感冒的
機會減到最小。

The politician tried to *minimize* his
role in the scandal when he was
questioned by the press.
這名政客在面對記者的詢問時，極力將
自己在這件醜聞中所扮演的角色，說得
極不重要。

minimum ﹝'mɪnəməm﹞
n. 最低限度　*adj.* 最低的

What is the *minimum* passing grade
for this course?
這門課的及格分數最低是幾分？

minor ﹝'maɪnɚ﹞*n.*
未成年者

It is illegal for *minors* to buy
cigarettes or alcohol.
未成年者購買煙酒是違法的。

minute ﹝maɪ'njut﹞
adj. 微小的

Even a *minute* amount of blood can
provide a sample of your DNA.
即使是少量的血，都可以提供你的 DNA
樣本。

mirror (ˈmɪrɚ) *n.* 鏡子

Before going out, he looked in the *mirror* to make sure his tie was straight.　他在出門前照了鏡子，以確認領帶是平直的。

misplace (mɪsˈples)
v. 忘記將…放在哪裡；
將…放錯位置

I must have *misplaced* my keys. They are not where I usually put them. 我一定是把鑰匙放錯地方了。它們不在我平常擺放鑰匙的地方。

miss (mɪs) *v.* 想念

It is not unusual to *miss* your family and friends during the first week of training.
在訓練期的第一週，想念家人和朋友是很正常的。

missile (ˈmɪsl̩) *n.* 飛彈

The military tested the *missile* by firing it into the sea.
軍方將飛彈發射到海裡作測試。

mission (ˈmɪʃən) *n.*
任務；使命

It is your *mission* to complete the report by tomorrow.
在明天完成報告是你的任務。

The charity has stated that its *mission* is to help the homeless.
這個慈善機構說，它們的使命是幫助無家可歸的人。

model (ˈmadl̩) *n.* 型；
模型

The manufacturer plans to introduce a new *model* of aircraft by the end of the year.
製造商打算在年底，引進新型的飛機。

The children are building *model* boats in the craft class.
孩子們在工藝課製作模型船。

moderate (ˈmadərɪt)
adj. 適中的

This store is too expensive; let's try to find one with more *moderate* prices. 這家店太貴了；我們再試著找一家價格較為適中的。

modern (ˈmadən)
adj. 現代化的

Many *modern* buildings are skyscrapers because land is much more expensive now than it was in the past. 許多現代化的建築都是摩天大樓，因為土地比以前貴多了。

moisture (ˈmɔɪstʃə)
n. 濕氣；水分

There is not enough *moisture* in the desert for this plant to survive there.
沙漠裡沒有足夠的水分，讓這種植物在那裡存活。

molecule (ˈmaləˌkjul)
n. 分子

How many atoms does a *molecule* of water contain?
一個水分子裡面，包含了多少個原子？

monitor 〔'mɑnətə 〕
n. 電腦螢幕   *v.* 監視

Don't forget to turn off the *monitor* when you are finished with the computer.
當你用完電腦時，不要忘記把螢幕關掉。

The patient was admitted to the hospital so that the doctor could *monitor* his progress. 這位病人被送入醫院治療，讓醫生能監視他的病情發展。

mop 〔 mɑp 〕 *v.* 拖地

One of your responsibilities is to *mop* the hall every day.
你其中一個責任，是每天用拖把將走廊的地拖一遍。

morale 〔 mo'ræl 〕 *n.* 士氣

As the strike continued, the *morale* of the workers began to fall. 由於罷工持續進行，所以工人們的士氣開始下降。

moreover 〔 mor'ovə 〕 *adv.* 此外

This apartment is too expensive. *Moreover*, it is too small for us.
這間公寓太貴了。此外，對我們而言太小了。

motion 〔'moʃən 〕 *n.* 搖動；動作

The *motion* of the boat made some of the passengers sick.
船的搖晃讓有些乘客感到不舒服。

mount ﹝maʊnt﹞ *v.*
騎上;安裝

It is easy for an experienced rider to *mount* a horse. 對一個經驗豐富的騎師而言,要騎上一匹馬是很容易的。

The photographer *mounted* the lens on the camera. 攝影師將鏡片裝上相機。

much ﹝mʌtʃ﹞ *adv.*
許多;大量

I'm afraid I don't know *much* about cars, so I can't help you fix it. 恐怕我對車子懂得不多,所以沒辦法幫你修。

muscle ﹝'mʌsḷ﹞ *n.* 肌肉

The doctor prescribed aspirin and rest for the pulled *muscle* in his leg. 醫生開了阿斯匹靈給他,並要他好好休息,以治療他腿部拉傷的肌肉。

muscular ﹝'mʌskjələ﹞
adj. 肌肉的;肌肉發達的

Many people are confined to wheelchairs by *muscular* diseases. 許多有肌肉疾病的人,都必須坐輪椅。

The *muscular* workers had no trouble lifting the heavy furniture. 肌肉發達的工人們,要抬起沉重的家具並不困難。

museum ﹝mju'ziəm﹞
n. 博物館

There is a special exhibit at the *museum* this month. 博物館在這個月有一個特別的展覽。

musical 〔ˈmjuzɪkḷ〕
n. 音樂劇

Many tourists like to go to a theater and see a *musical* when they visit New York.
許多遊客到紐約玩時，喜歡到劇院看音樂劇。

musician 〔mjuˈzɪʃən〕
n. 音樂家

An orchestra is composed of many *musicians*.
管絃樂團是由許多音樂家所組成的。

must 〔mʌst〕*aux.* 必定

John isn't here; he *must* be at the library.
約翰不在這裡；他一定是在圖書館。

mustache 〔ˈmʌstæʃ〕
n. (嘴唇上面的) 鬍子；髭

The thief had a *mustache* but no beard.
小偷嘴唇上留有鬍子，但下巴沒有。

mustard 〔ˈmʌstəd〕
n. 芥末

Billy doesn't like *mustard* on his hot dog; just give him ketchup.
比利不喜歡在熱狗上加芥末；只要給他蕃茄醬就好了。

N

nail (nel) *n.* 釘子

The carpenter used three *nails* to join the two boards.

木匠用三根釘子把這兩塊木板接合。

nap (næp) *n.* 午睡

In some countries it is common for people to take a *nap* in the afternoon.

在某些國家，人們在下午睡個午覺是很常見的。

nation ('neʃən) *n.* 國家

The flag of this *nation* is quite different from our flag.

這個國家的國旗，和我們的大不相同。

national ('næʃənḷ)
adj. 全國性的

The government set up a *national* program to provide better health care for people all over the country.

政府制定了一項計劃，以提供全國人民更完善的醫療保健服務。

nature ('netʃə) *n.* 本性

Mrs. Cooper has a very forgiving *nature* and she never holds a grudge.

庫培太太天性非常寬容，而且從不懷恨在心。

navigate (ˈnævɪˌget)
v. 領航；導航

This map will help you to *navigate*.
這幅地圖對你的導航有幫助。

```
nav +  ig  + ate
 |      |     |
ship + drive +  v.
```

navigator
(ˈnævəˌgetɚ) *n.* 領航員

The *navigator* informed us that we had been blown off course during the storm. 領航員通知我們，我們在暴風雨中，被吹離了航線。

neat (nit) *adj.* 整潔的；
愛乾淨的

She is a very *neat* person and always keeps her room in good order.
她是個很愛乾淨的人，總是把房間保持得很整齊。

necessary (ˈnɛsəˌsɛrɪ)
adj. 必要的

If you want to see this movie, it is *necessary* to buy tickets in advance.
如果你要看這部電影，就必須事先買票。

needle (ˈnidḷ) *n.* 針

The sick man refused to have an injection because he is afraid of *needles*.
這位病人拒絕打針，因為他害怕針。

negative (ˈnɛgətɪv) *adj.*
負的；陰極的

One end of the battery has a *negative* charge. 電池的一端是負電荷。

neglect 〔 nɪ'glɛkt 〕 *v.*
忽視；忘了做

The dog was ***neglected*** by its owner.
這隻狗被牠的主人忽視。

I ***neglected*** to lock the door when I
went out. 我出門時忘了鎖門。

neighborhood
〔'nebɚ,hud 〕 *n.* 鄰近地區

We find our new ***neighborhood*** much
quieter than where we lived before.
我們發現我們新搬來的這一區，比以前住
的地方安靜多了。

neither 〔'niðɚ 〕 *adj.*
兩者皆非

The red watch is too large and the
gold one is too small, but the black
one is ***neither***; it's just right.
紅色的錶太大，而金色的太小，但是黑色
的錶則不大也不小，剛剛好。

nerve 〔 nɝv 〕 *n.* 神經

A patient with ***nerve*** damage may not
be able to feel pain.
神經受損的病人，可能感覺不到痛。

network 〔'nɛt,wɝk 〕
n. 網狀組織

Although the city has a good ***network***
of roads, there is still heavy traffic
during rush hour.
雖然這個城市有完善的道路網，但尖峰時
間仍有交通擁擠的狀況。

nitrogen (ˈnaɪtrədʒən)
n. 氮氣

Nitrogen is an important element of the earth's atmosphere.
氮氣是地球大氣層中的重要元素。

nominate (ˈnɑmə͵net)
v. 提名

Which politician do you think the party will *nominate* for president?
你覺得這個政黨會提名哪一位政治家當總統呢？

nonetheless
(͵nʌnðəˈlɛs) adv.
儘管如此

We were exhausted after the game, but we had to clean the house *nonetheless*.
我們在比完賽後都很累，但儘管如此，還是得把房子清理乾淨。

normal (ˈnɔrml̩) adj.
正常的

During the heat wave, the temperature was far above *normal*.
在熱浪來襲期間，溫度遠高於常溫。

note (not) n. 短箋

I left a *note* for Helen to let her know that we are going swimming after class today.
我留了一張短箋給海倫，讓她知道我們今天下課後要去游泳。

notice (ˈnotɪs) v.
注意到

Helen *noticed* that he did not feel well and told him to see a doctor.
海倫注意到他不舒服，叫他要去看醫生。

nowadays (ˈnauəˌdez)
adv. 現在

Knowledge of computers is very important *nowadays*.
現在電腦方面的知識很重要。

nowhere (ˈnoˌhwɛr)
adv. 什麼地方都沒有

I was tired, but there was *nowhere* to sit down.
我累了，但是沒有地方可以坐下來。

nuclear (ˈnjuklɪə)
adj. 核子的

The residents protested against the plan to build a *nuclear* power plant because they were afraid of the effects of atomic power.
居民們抗議興建核電廠的計劃，因為他們害怕原子能會產生的影響。

numb (nʌm) *adj.*
麻木的

My mouth felt *numb* for hours after I left the dentist.
在離開牙醫幾個小時後，我的嘴巴還覺得麻。

numerous
(ˈnjumərəs) *adj.* 許多的

There are *numerous* books in the library that I have not read.
圖書館裡有許多我沒看過的書。

O

object ﹝ əb'dʒɛkt ﹞ v.
反對 < to >

I *object* to your proposal because it
is not practical. 我反對你的計劃,因為
那是不切實際的。

```
  ob   +  ject
  |       |
against + throw
```

objective ﹝ əb'dʒɛktɪv ﹞
adj. 客觀的

It is difficult to be *objective* about
your own shortcomings.
要客觀地看待你自己的缺點,是很困難的。

obligation
﹝ͺɑblə'geʃən ﹞ n. 義務;
責任

You have an *obligation* to take care
of your family.
你有義務要照顧你的家庭。

observation
﹝ͺɑbzɚ'veʃən ﹞ n. 觀察

After watching the old man for a
while, she made the *observation* that
he was very energetic for his age.
在注視這個老人一會兒之後,她觀察到,
以老人的年齡來說,他算是精力非常充
沛的。

observe ﹝ əb'zɝv ﹞ v.
遵守

If you don't *observe* the rules, you
will be fined.
如果你不遵守這些規則,
你將被處以罰款。

```
ob + serve
|     |
to  + keep
```

obsolete ('ɑbsə,lit)
adj. 落伍的

The spread of computers has made manual typewriters seem *obsolete*. 電腦的普及，使得用手操作的打字機，看起來十分落伍。

obstacle ('ɑbstəkḷ)
n. 阻礙；障礙

The fact that she did not complete high school is an *obstacle* in her search for a job. 她未完成高中學業的事實，是她找工作的一個阻礙。

ob	+	sta	+	cle
against	+	stand	+	*n.*

The recruits were asked to run an *obstacle* course as part of their training. 新兵們被要求去跑超越障礙訓練場，這是他們訓練的一部份。

obstruct (əb'strʌkt)
v. 妨礙

Park your car at the side of the road so that you do not *obstruct* traffic. 把你的車停在路邊，這樣才不會妨礙交通。

ob	+	struct
against	+	build

obtain (əb'ten) *v.* 獲得

The students caught cheating were able to *obtain* the answers before the test. 被抓到作弊的學生，有辦法在考試前獲得解答。

ob	+	tain
near	+	hold

obvious (ˈɑbvɪəs)
adj. 明顯的

It's ***obvious*** from your expression that you are upset. What's wrong? 從你的表情可以明顯知道你不高興。怎麼了？

occasion (əˈkeʒən)
n. 場合；特別的大事

Weddings, birthdays and anniversaries are special ***occasions***.
婚禮、生日，以及週年紀念日，都是特別的大事。

occupy (ˈɑkjəˌpaɪ) *v.*
佔據；填滿

If you are bored, find something to ***occupy*** your time.
如果你覺得無聊，找點事來填滿你的時間。

```
oc + cupy
 |     |
at + seize
```

occur (əˈkɝ) *v.* 發生

When did the argument ***occur***?
這次的爭論是什麼時候發生的？

offense (əˈfɛns) *n.*
攻擊；違規；犯法行爲

We lost the game because the other team's ***offense*** was very strong.
因爲對方球隊的攻勢很強，所以我們輸了這場比賽。

Running through a red light is a traffic ***offense***. 闖紅燈是一種交通違規。

official (əˈfɪʃəl)
adj. 正式的

Our graduation was an ***official*** ceremony.
我們的畢業典禮是非常正式的典禮。

opera〔'ɑpərə〕*n.* 歌劇

I enjoyed both the music and the story of the *opera.*

那齣歌劇中的音樂和故事,我都很喜歡。

operate〔'ɑpə,ret〕*v.*
動手術

The patient's condition was so serious that the doctor decided to *operate* right away.

這位病人的情況非常嚴重,
所以醫生決定馬上動手術。

```
oper + ate
 |      |
work +  v.
```

opportunity
〔,ɑpə'tjunətɪ〕*n.* 機會

The students who failed were glad to have the *opportunity* to take the test again. 考不及格的學生,很高興能有機會再考一次。

oppose〔ə'poz〕*v.* 反對

My parents *oppose* my plan to find a part-time job.

我爸媽反對我找兼職工作的計劃。

```
op   + pose
 |      |
against + put
```

opposite〔'ɑpəzɪt〕
prep. 在～對面

The post office is *opposite* the bank.

郵局在銀行的對面。

optional〔'ɑpʃənḷ〕*adj.*
非強制的

The meeting is *optional,* so I choose not to attend. 這場會議不是強制參加的,所以我選擇不出席。

orchestra (ˈɔrkɪstrə)
n. 管絃樂團

The *orchestra* gave a wonderful concert last night. 這個管絃樂團昨晚所舉行的音樂會非常精采。

orderly (ˈɔrdəlɪ) *adj.*
整齊的

Please arrange the books on the shelves in an *orderly* way.
請將書整齊地排在架子上。

ordinary (ˈɔrdn͵ɛrɪ)
adj. 平常的

The bridge is closed today, so we cannot take the *ordinary* way to work.
橋樑今天封閉，所以我們無法走平常的路去上班。

ore (or) *n.* 礦石

The miners found a great deal of *ore* in the new mine.
礦工在新的礦坑發現了大量的礦石。

organ (ˈɔrgən) *n.*
器官；風琴

The heart is a vital *organ*.
心臟是維持生命所必需的器官。

Stephen plays the *organ* in church on Sundays.
史蒂芬每個星期天都在教堂彈風琴。

origin (ˈɔrədʒɪn) *n.*
起源；來源

The *origin* of the flight arriving at gate 12 was Hong Kong.
到達第十二號登機門的班機，是來自香港的。

original ﹝ əˋrɪdʒən! ﹞
adj. 原來的；最初的

The *original* owner of the house moved overseas.
這房子原來的屋主搬到海外去了。

otherwise ﹝ˋʌðəˏwaɪz ﹞
adv. 否則

Remember to lock your car; *otherwise*, it might be stolen.
記得把車上鎖；否則它可能會被偷。

outer ﹝ˋautə ﹞ *adj.*
外面的

When you are in the mountains, your *outer* layer of clothing should protect you from the wind.
當你在山上的時候，你的外層衣物應該要能防風。

outfit ﹝ˋautˏfɪt ﹞
n. 公司；企業
v. 配備；供給

This company is a reputable *outfit*; it is unlikely that they would try to cheat you. 這是一家聲譽卓著的公司，他們不太可能欺騙你。

This store can *outfit* you with everything you need to go camping.
這家店能提供你去露營所需的一切裝備。

output ﹝ˋautˏput ﹞ *n.*
產量

The new machinery will increase the factory's *output* so we will be able to supply more of our products to stores.
新的機器將會增加工廠的產量，所以我們將可以提供更多產品給商店。

outside (ˈaʊtˈsaɪd)
adv. 在戶外

We usually go on a picnic on Sunday because we enjoy eating *outside*.
我們通常星期天去野餐，因爲我們喜歡在戶外吃東西。

overall (ˌovəˈɔl) *adv.*
大體上；就整體來說

Although the student missed three questions on the exam, he did well *overall*.
雖然這位學生在考試中看漏了三條題目，他整體來說考得很好。

overcome (ˌovəˈkʌm)
v. 克服

The fisherman quit his job because he was unable to *overcome* his fear of water.
這位漁夫辭掉了他的工作，因爲他無法克服對水的恐懼。

overseas (ˈovəˈsiz)
adv. 到國外

We need to get a passport before we go *overseas*.
我們在出國前，必須先拿到護照。

oxygen (ˈɑksədʒən)
n. 氧氣

The doctor gave the patient *oxygen* in order to help him breathe more easily. 醫生給病人氧氣，以幫助他呼吸更順暢。

P

paint 〔 pent 〕 *v.* 油漆

The house is in good condition, but we need to *paint* the outside of it.

這棟房子的屋況良好,但我們需要油漆一下外面。

panel 〔'pænḷ 〕 *n.* (汽車、飛機等的) 儀表板

The airplane's control *panel* is located in the cockpit.

控制飛機的儀表板位於駕駛艙內。

parade 〔 pə'red 〕 *n.* 遊行;閱兵

On National Day, our country celebrates with a *parade* and fireworks.

在國慶日,我國是以遊行和煙火來慶祝。

participate 〔 par'tɪsə͵pet 〕 *v.* 參加 < *in* >

The athlete was not allowed to *participate* in the race because he tested positive for drugs.

這名運動員不得參加這場比賽,因為他的藥物檢驗結果是呈陽性反應。

```
parti + cipate
  |       |
part  +  take
```

particle 〔'partɪkḷ 〕 *n.* 粒子

Susan could not see clearly because she had a *particle* of dust in her eye.

蘇珊看不清楚,因為她的眼睛裡有一粒沙子。

particular ﹙pə'tɪkjələ﹚
adj. 特定的;特別的

In general, the prices in this store are reasonable, but this *particular* dress is expensive.
一般來說,這家店的價格合理,但這件洋裝卻很貴。

passenger ﹙'pæsn̩dʒə﹚
n. 乘客

The train conductor asked the *passengers* to show him their tickets.
火車上的管理員要求乘客向他出示車票。

path ﹙pæθ﹚ *n.* 小路;路線

You can follow this *path* to the river.
你可以沿著這條小路走到河那邊。

patience ﹙'peʃəns﹚ *n.* 耐心

Rita did not have enough *patience* to wait in the long line at the post office. 麗塔沒有足夠的耐心,在郵局大排長龍地等待。

patient ﹙'peʃənt﹚ *adj.* 有耐心的

George tried to be *patient* while waiting in the traffic jam.
喬治試著要在塞車時耐心地等待。

peak ﹙pik﹚ *n.* 山頂

We were happy to reach the *peak* of the mountain after such a long and tiring climb.
在經過長時間而且令人疲倦的攀登過程後,我們很高興能到達山頂。

penetrate (ˈpɛnəˌtret)
v. 刺穿；貫穿

I stepped on a nail, but luckily it did not *penetrate* my skin. 我踩到了一根釘子，但很幸運的，並沒有刺穿我的皮膚。

penicillin (ˌpɛnɪˈsɪlɪn)
n. 盤尼西林

Penicillin is an important drug in the treatment of many diseases.
在治療許多疾病時，盤尼西林是一種很重要的藥。

per (pɚ) *prep.* 每

This is a sparsely populated region with only ten people *per* square mile.
這是一個人口稀少的地區，每平方英哩只有十個人。

perfect (ˈpɝfɪkt) *adj.*
完美的；理想的

This apartment is *perfect* for us because it is close to my office.
這棟公寓對我們而言非常理想，因為它離我的辦公室很近。

per	+ fect
thoroughly	+ *make*

perform (pɚˈfɔrm)
v. 執行；表演

The policeman had no choice but to *perform* his duty and arrest his own son when he saw him steal the car.
這位警察在看見自己的兒子偷車時，沒有選擇的餘地，只能盡他的責任，將他逮捕。

per	+ form
thoroughly	+ *provide*

performance

〔 pəˋfɔrməns 〕 *n.* 表演

The singer gave a wonderful *performance* and the audience clapped loudly.

這位歌手的表演非常精采，所以觀眾們大聲地鼓掌。

period 〔ˋpɪrɪəd 〕 *n.*
期間

The criminal was sent to prison for a *period* of ten years.

這個罪犯坐了十年的牢。

periodic 〔͵pɪrɪˋɑdɪk 〕
adj. 定期的

The airplane must be given *periodic* maintenance in order to be safe to fly.

為了飛行安全起見，飛機必須要定期維修。

periodically

〔͵pɪrɪˋɑdɪkḷɪ 〕 *adv.* 定期地

The students' progress will be tested *periodically*.

學生們的進步情形，將被定期測驗。

permanent

〔ˋpɝmənənt 〕 *adj.* 永久的

The stain is *permanent*; you cannot wash it out.

這是個永久的污點；你無法將它洗掉。

personality

〔͵pɝsṇˋælətɪ 〕 *n.* 性格；
個性

My brother has a very generous *personality*; he is always helping others.

我哥哥的個性非常慷慨；他總是會幫助別人。

personnel (ˌpɜsn'ɛl)
n. 全體職員

The *personnel* of this company are upset over the pay cuts. 這家公司的職員，對於被減薪，非常不高興。

perspire (pə'spaɪr)
v. 流汗　同 *sweat*

The heat of the auditorium made us *perspire*.
大禮堂很熱，使我們都流汗了。

pertain (pə'ten) *v.*
有關＜*to*＞

What did Mr. Smith's phone call *pertain* to?
史密斯先生打電話來，是關於什麼事？

petroleum
(pə'troliəm) *n.* 石油

One important source of fuel is *petroleum*.
石油是燃料的重要來源之一。

pharmacist
('fɑrməsɪst) *n.* 藥劑師

A *pharmacist* must be very careful when preparing medications.
藥劑師在配藥時，必須非常小心。

pharmacy ('fɑrməsɪ)
n. 藥局

I have to buy this medicine at the *pharmacy*.
我必須到藥局去買這種藥。

phase (fez) *n.* 階段

The bridge is in the last *phase* of construction; it will be finished soon.
這座橋已進入工程的最後階段；很快就會完工了。

photo (ˈfoto) *n.* 照片

We enjoyed looking at the ***photos*** Jessica took on her vacation.

我們愉快地看著潔西卡在渡假時拍的照片。

physical (ˈfɪzɪkl̩) *adj.* 身體的

It is important to go to the doctor for a ***physical*** exam when you do not feel well.

當你感到不舒服時，去看醫生做個身體檢查，是很重要的。

piano (pɪˈæno) *n.* 鋼琴

Brian has been studying the ***piano*** since he was a child. It's no wonder that he can play so well.

布萊恩從小就開始學鋼琴。難怪他可以彈得這麼好。

pickle (ˈpɪkl̩) *n.* 泡菜

I didn't put any ***pickles*** in the salad because Jane doesn't like them.

我沒有在沙拉中放任何泡菜，因為珍不喜歡。

picnic (ˈpɪknɪk) *n.* 野餐

The sun is shining so it's a good day for a ***picnic***.

陽光普照，所以今天是野餐的好天氣。

pile (paɪl) *n.* 一堆

The gardener raked the leaves into a big ***pile***. 園丁將樹葉耙成大大的一堆。

pill 〔 pɪl 〕 *n.* 藥丸

The nurse gave me some *pills* for my headache.
護士給了我一些治療頭痛的藥丸。

pin 〔 pɪn 〕 *n.* 別針

The salesclerk used a *pin* to attach his name tag.
售貨員用別針將他的名牌別上。

plain 〔 plen 〕 *adj.* 清楚的;易懂的

The expression on your face makes it *plain* that you don't like the food.
從你臉上的表情可以清楚地知道,你不喜歡這種食物。

plant 〔 plænt 〕 *n.* 工廠;植物

The *plant* will be closed because there is not enough demand for the goods it produces.
這座工廠即將關閉,因為所生產的商品,需求量不足。

pleasure 〔'plɛʒɚ〕 *n.* 樂趣;快樂的事

It was a *pleasure* to relax after the long trip.
在長途旅行後,放鬆一下是件快樂的事。

pliers 〔'plaɪɚz〕 *n.pl.* 鉗子

Hand me the *pliers*; I want to bend this wire.
把鉗子拿給我;我要把這條鐵絲弄彎。

plot ﹝plɑt﹞ *v.*
繪製路線

With the help of the compass, we were able to *plot* our course through the mountains. 有了指南針的協助，我們才能繪製穿越山區的路線。

poison ﹝'pɔɪzn̩﹞ *n.*
毒藥

In order to kill the rats, we put out some *poison*.
爲了滅鼠，我們拿出一些毒藥。

poisonous ﹝'pɔɪznəs﹞
adj. 有毒的

If you are bitten by a *poisonous* snake, it is important to get medical help immediately. 如果你被毒蛇咬到，最重要的是，要立刻就醫治療。

pole ﹝pol﹞ *n.* 極；
極地

Both the North *Pole* and the South *Pole* have extreme climates.
北極和南極的氣候都非常極端。

polish ﹝'pɑlɪʃ﹞ *v.* 擦亮

Remember to *polish* your boots before the inspection.
記得在檢查前，擦亮你的靴子。

pollute ﹝pə'lut﹞ *v.*
污染

The residents do not want a new factory in their neighborhood because they are afraid it would *pollute* the environment.
居民們不想要新工廠建在他們附近，因爲他們害怕工廠會污染環境。

poorly (ˈpʊrlɪ) *adv.*
不充分地；差勁地

I slept *poorly* last night because I drank too much coffee.
因為喝了太多咖啡，所以我昨晚睡眠不足。

populate (ˈpɑpjəˌlet)
v. 居住於

This neighborhood is largely *populated* by immigrants from Latin America.
這附近的居民，大部份都是拉丁美洲來的移民。

population
(ˌpɑpjəˈleʃən) *n.* 人口

The *population* of a country can be measured by taking a census.
一國的人口，可以利用人口普查來計算。

port (port) *n.* 港口
adj. 左舷的

When will the ship leave *port*?
船何時要出港？

We stood on the *port* side of the ship to see the whale.
我們站在船的左舷賞鯨。

portable (ˈportəb!)
adj. 手提的

Tim carries a *portable* radio when he goes jogging.
當提姆去慢跑時，會帶著手提式的收音機。

portion (ˈporʃən) *n.*
部分

We ate a *portion* of the cake and saved the rest for later.
我們吃了一部份的蛋糕，然後把剩下的留到稍後再吃。

position (pəˈzɪʃən)
n. 職位;姿勢

Harry was promoted to the *position* of vice-president last week.
哈利上週升上了副總裁的職位。

I had to sit in an uncomfortable *position* on the plane and now my back hurts. 因為在飛機上必須以不舒服的姿勢坐著,所以我的背現在很痛。

positive (ˈpɑzətɪv)
adj. 正的;陽的

One end of the battery has a *positive* charge and the other has a negative one. 電池的一端是正電荷,另一端則是負電荷。

possible (ˈpɑsəbḷ)
adj. 可能的

Is it *possible* to send an astronaut to Mars? 有可能把太空人送到火星上嗎?

possibly (ˈpɑsəblɪ)
adv. 可能地

The train cannot *possibly* have arrived. It's not due until 2:30.
火車不可能已經到站了。它應該是兩點半才會到。

postpone (postˈpon)
v. 延期

We had to *postpone* the fireworks because of rain.
因為下雨,我們必須延期施放煙火。

post + pone
after + put

potential 〔 pəˈtɛnʃəl 〕
n. 潛力

John is a gifted student and has the *potential* to be an outstanding scientist. 約翰是個有天賦的學生,而且有成爲傑出科學家的潛力。

pour 〔 por 〕 *v.* 傾倒

Please *pour* some tea for everyone. 請倒些茶給每個人。

powder 〔ˈpaʊdɚ 〕 *n.*
粉末;火藥

The student had traces of gun *powder* on his hands. 這名學生的手上有少許的砲灰。

power 〔ˈpaʊɚ 〕 *n.*
力;力量

The electric *power* was cut off during the storm. 電力在暴風雨期間被切斷了。

powerful 〔ˈpaʊɚfəl 〕
adj. 強有力的

A jet requires a *powerful* engine. 噴射機需要有強力的引擎。

practical 〔ˈpræktɪkl̩ 〕
adj. 實用的

It is *practical* to own a car in the United States. 在美國,擁有一部車是很實用的。

precaution
〔 prɪˈkɔʃən 〕 *n.* 預防措施

When a typhoon is approaching, we must take *precautions* in order to prevent damage to our homes. 當颱風接近的時候,我們必須採取預防措施,以防止颱風對我們的家園造成損害。

precede ﹝ prɪˊsid ﹞
v. 在…之前

The flag ceremony will *precede* the speeches.
演講之前，會先舉行升旗典禮。

precipitation
﹝ prɪͺsɪpəˊteʃən ﹞ *n.* 降雨

The weather center predicts that there will be some *precipitation* tomorrow, so we may have to hold the ceremony inside.
氣象中心預測明天會下雨，所以我們可能必須在室內舉行典禮。

precise ﹝ prɪˊsaɪs ﹞
adj. 精確的

Please give me a *precise* account of the company's financial situation.
請向我精確說明這家公司的財務狀況。

```
pre  + cise
 |       |
before + cut
```

prefer ﹝ prɪˊfɝ ﹞ *v.*
比較喜歡

He would *prefer* to see a comedy because he does not like sad movies.
他會比較喜歡看喜劇，因為他不喜歡悲傷的電影。

```
pre  + fer
 |       |
before + carry
```

preference
﹝ˊprɛfərəns ﹞ *n.* 偏愛

Tom has a *preference* for name-brand clothes.
湯姆偏愛名牌服飾。

prescribe 〔 prɪ'skraɪb 〕
v. 開藥方

You cannot buy this drug over the counter; a doctor must *prescribe* it for you. 沒有醫師的處方籤，你不能買這種藥；必須有醫生替你開藥方才行。

present 〔'prɛzn̩t 〕 *n.*
禮物

We usually give *presents* to people on their birthdays.
我們通常會在人們生日時送禮物。

preserve 〔 prɪ'zɝv 〕
v. 保存

We cannot possibly eat all these tomatoes; we will have to *preserve* some of them. 我們不可能將這些蕃茄全吃光；我們必須將其中一些保存起來。

```
pre    + serve
 |        |
beforehand + keep
```

press 〔 prɛs 〕 *v.* 按

Frank *pressed* the button to call the elevator.
法蘭克按了按鈕，要搭電梯。

pretty 〔'prɪtɪ 〕 *adv.*
相當；非常

I am *pretty* sure that class begins at 9:00. 我非常確定是九點開始上課。

prevent 〔 prɪ'vɛnt 〕
v. 預防<*from*>

Be sure to lock your bicycle to *prevent* someone from stealing it.
要確定你的腳踏車上鎖了，以防止有人把它偷走。

preventable
〔 prɪˋvɛntəb! 〕 *adj.*
可預防的

Measles is a *preventable* disease, but you need to be vaccinated.
麻疹是可以預防的疾病,但你必須要接種疫苗。

previous 〔ˋprivɪəs 〕
adj. 先前的

Sally's *previous* school was in Boston. She moved here last year.
莎莉先前的學校是在波士頓。她去年搬到這裡。

```
pre  +  vi  + ous
 |       |     |
before + way +  adj.
```

prime 〔 praɪm 〕 *adj.*
最好的

Traffic jams are a *prime* example of the problems that come with living in a city. 因為住在城市而產生的問題中,交通阻塞是最好的例子。

primitive 〔ˋprɪmətɪv 〕
adj. 原始的

Before the development of agriculture, man lived a very *primitive* life.
在發展農業之前,人類過著非常原始的生活。

principal 〔ˋprɪnsəp! 〕
adj. 主要的　*n.* 校長

The *principal* goal of the committee is to select a new chairperson.
這個委員會的主要目標,是選出新的主席。

The *principal* decided to cancel the school picnic.
校長決定要將校內野餐取消。

principle〔ˈprɪnsəpl̩〕
n. 原則

It is against my *principles* to lie.
說謊違背我的原則。

print〔prɪnt〕*v.* 列印

I will *print* two copies of my report.
我會把我的報告印出兩份副本。

printer〔ˈprɪntɚ〕*n.*
印表機

This *printer* makes very clear copies.
這台印表機可以印出非常清晰的副本。

prior〔ˈpraɪɚ〕*adj.*
之前的

I'm afraid I can't have lunch with
you; I have a *prior* appointment.
我恐怕不能和你一起吃午餐；我之前已和
別人約好了。

prison〔ˈprɪzn̩〕*n.* 監獄

The murderer was sentenced to life
in *prison*.
那名兇手被判終身監禁。

prisoner〔ˈprɪznɚ〕
n. 囚犯

The *prisoner* was released early
because of his good behavior.
這名囚犯因表現良好而提前獲釋。

privacy〔ˈpraɪvəsɪ〕
n. 隱私權

The press often does not respect the
privacy of celebrities.
新聞界常不尊重名人的隱私。

private 〔'praɪvɪt 〕
adj. 私人的

The tennis courts belong to a *private* club; you must be a member in order to use them.

這些網球場是屬於私人俱樂部所有；你必須是會員，才能使用。

privilege 〔'prɪvḷɪdʒ 〕
n. 特權

I am not a member of that club, so I do not have the *privilege* of playing tennis there.

我不是那個俱樂部的會員，所以沒有在那邊打網球的特權。

```
privi  + lege
  |        |
private +  law
```

probably 〔'prɑbəblɪ 〕
adv. 可能

We will *probably* be late because of the heavy traffic.

因爲交通很擁擠，我們可能會遲到。

procedure
〔 prə'sidʒɚ 〕 *n.* 程序

What is the correct *procedure* for filing an application?

提出申請的正確程序是什麼？

proceed 〔 prə'sid 〕
v. 前進；繼續進行

We were told to *proceed* to the classroom after registering.

有人告訴我們，在註冊後就前往教室。

After the rain delay, the game *proceeded*.

在被雨耽擱之後，比賽繼續進行。

produce 〔 prəˈdjus 〕
v. 生產；製造

The factory will continue to *produce* automotive parts despite the slow economy. 儘管經濟不景氣，這家工廠還是會繼續生產汽車零件。

```
pro   + duce
 |        |
forward + lead
```

product 〔ˈprɑdʌkt 〕
n. 產品

These handicrafts are a *product* of this region. 這些手工藝品是這個地區的產品。

production
〔 prəˈdʌkʃən 〕 *n.* 生產

The Middle East is known for its *production* of oil. 中東以出產石油聞名。

proficient
〔 prəˈfɪʃənt 〕 *adj.* 精通的

He is a talented athlete and is *proficient* at several sports. 他是一個有才能的運動員，而且精通好幾種運動項目。

```
pro   + fici + ent
 |       |      |
forward + make + adj.
```

progress 〔ˈprɑgrɛs 〕
n. 進步
〔 prəˈgrɛs 〕 *v.* 進步

My son has made a lot of *progress* in reading. 我的兒子在閱讀方面進步很多。

```
pro   + gress
 |        |
forward + walk
```

If you continue to work hard, you will continue to *progress*.
如果你繼續努力，你就會持續進步。

prohibit 〔 proˈhɪbɪt 〕
v. 妨礙；禁止

The traffic jam *prohibited* us from getting to the concert on time.
交通阻塞使我們無法準時到達音樂會。

The city government *prohibits* swimming in the lake. 市政府禁止在這個湖裡游泳。

project 〔ˈprɑdʒɛkt 〕
n. 計劃

We must complete the science *project* by the end of this semester. 我們必須在這學期結束前，完成這個科學計劃。

promise 〔ˈprɑmɪs 〕
v. 承諾

You must *promise* not to make this mistake again.
你必須承諾，不會再犯這樣的錯誤。

```
pro + mise
 |     |
forth + send
```

promote 〔 prəˈmot 〕
v. 使升遷

If you work hard, your boss will *promote* you.
如果你努力工作，你的老闆將會讓你升職。

```
pro  + mote
 |      |
forward + move
```

promotion
〔 prəˈmoʃən 〕 *n.* 升遷

Diane just received a *promotion*; she is now a second lieutenant.
黛安剛升職；她現在是少尉。

propel 〔 prəˈpɛl 〕 *v.*
推進

We *propel* a bicycle by pedaling it.
我們踩腳踏車的踏板，使它前進。

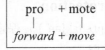

```
pro  + pel
 |     |
forward + drive
```

propeller 〔 prəˈpɛlɚ 〕
n. 推進器

A helicopter depends on a *propeller* to keep it in the air.
直昇機是靠推進器，使它停留在空中。

proper 〔ˈprɑpɚ 〕 *adj.*
正確的；適當的

That is not the *proper* way to use the microscope.
這不是使用顯微鏡的正確方法。

properly 〔ˈprɑpɚlɪ 〕
adv. 適當地

If you don't store the food *properly*, it may spoil.
如果你不適當地儲存食物，它可能會腐壞。

property 〔ˈprɑpɚtɪ 〕
n. 特性

One *property* of this flower is its unusual smell.
這種花的特性之一，就是味道很不尋常。

protection
〔 prɛˈtɛkʃən 〕 *n.* 保護；
防禦

Daniel used an umbrella as *protection* against the rain.
丹尼爾用雨傘擋雨。

protrude 〔 proˈtrud 〕
v. 突出

You should park your car more carefully; it is *protruding* into the street. 你停車時應該要更小心一點；你的車突出在街道上了。

pro	+	trude
forth	+	*thrust*

proud 〔 praʊd 〕 *adj.*
光榮的

You should be ***proud*** of yourself for winning the race.
你應該為自己贏得比賽感到光榮。

proudly 〔'praʊdlɪ 〕
adv. 得意地

The man spoke ***proudly*** about his grandson's accomplishments.
這個男人得意地談論他孫子的成就。

prove 〔 pruv 〕 *v.* 證明

We hope that this experiment will ***prove*** our theory.
我們希望這個實驗,能證明我們的理論。

provided (that)
〔 prə'vaɪdɪd 〕 *conj.* 如果

I will lend you the money ***provided*** that you repay it by Friday.
如果你在星期五以前還錢,我就把錢借給你。

providing (that)
〔 prə'vaɪdɪŋ 〕 *conj.* 如果

Providing that the train leaves on time, we should arrive at 6:00.
如果火車準時出發,我們應該會在六點到達。

public 〔'pʌblɪk 〕 *adj.*
公共的

This is a ***public*** swimming pool; anyone may enter.
這是一個公共游泳池;任何人都可以進入。

publish 〔'pʌblɪʃ 〕 *v.*
出版

The writer is trying to ***publish*** his latest book.
這名作家試著要出版他最新的書。

pull 〔 pul 〕 *v.*
把（肌肉、腱等）拉傷

I *pulled* a muscle while playing basketball, and now it is difficult for me to walk. 我在打籃球的時候拉傷了肌肉，所以現在走路有困難。

pulse 〔 pʌls 〕 *n.* 脈搏

As part of the examination, the doctor took my *pulse*.
醫生為我量脈搏，這是檢查的一部份。

punch 〔 pʌntʃ 〕 *v.*
打洞；毆打

The guard *punched* a hole in the box to see what was inside.
警衛在盒子上打個洞，看看裡面是什麼。

If you *punch* someone, you will be sent to the principal's office.
如果你毆打別人，你將會被送到校長室去。

pure 〔 pjur 〕 *adj.* 純粹的

This sweater is made of *pure* wool; it's 100% wool. 這件毛衣是純羊毛製的；是百分之百的羊毛料。

puzzle 〔 'pʌzl̩ 〕 *n.* 難題

How to program a VCR is a *puzzle* to many people.
要如何拍攝一段 VCR，對許多人而言是個難題。

Q

quiet (ˈkwaɪət) *adj.*
安靜的

It is usually very *quiet* in the library.
圖書館通常都非常安靜。

quit (kwɪt) *v.* 停止

The teacher asked us to *quit* talking
because it was time to begin the test.
老師要我們停止說話,因為開始考試的時
間到了。

【劉毅老師的話】

　　軍事院校的學生,最大的優點是身體
好,語言表達能力強,如果將英文學好,
就很容易出人頭地。

R

radar ('redɑr) *n.* 雷達

The plane was flying too low to show up on the *radar*.
這架飛機飛得太低，以致於無法顯示在雷達上。

radiate ('redɪ,et) *v.* 發出（光、熱等）

The sun *radiates* both heat and light.
太陽發出光和熱。

radiation (,redɪ'eʃən) *n.* 放射

The *radiation* of light in a solar eclipse is too bright to look at; it will damage our eyes.
日蝕時所放射出的光太亮，使人無法直視；它會傷害我們的眼睛。

radiator ('redɪ,etɚ) *n.*（汽車引擎的）散熱器

The *radiator* was damaged in the car accident.
散熱器在車禍中受損了。

radioactive (,redɪo'æktɪv) *adj.* 有放射性的

The material used in making this bomb is *radioactive*.
用來製造這枚炸彈的材料，是具有放射性的。

raise (rez) *v.* 飼養；撫養

The brothers *raise* cattle on their ranch. 這對兄弟在他們的牧場養牛。

ranch ﹝ ræntʃ ﹞ *n.* 牧場

My family's *ranch* consists of one thousand acres.

我家的牧場，是由一千英畝的地所組成。

rancher ﹝ˈrentʃɚ﹞ *n.* 牧場主人

My uncle has been a *rancher* all his life; he can't imagine leaving the country.

我叔叔一輩子都是牧場主人；他無法想像離開鄉下的生活。

range ﹝ rendʒ ﹞ *n.* 範圍

The radio has a *range* of several hundred miles.

這個無線電能涵蓋數百英哩的範圍。

rapid ﹝ˈræpɪd﹞ *adj.* 迅速的

There was a *rapid* decrease in the number of traffic accidents after the new signs were put in place.

在適當的位置豎立了新的告示之後，車禍的數量便迅速地減少了。

rare ﹝ rɛr ﹞ *adj.* 罕見的；稀有的

The *rare* book is very expensive because it is not easy to find.

這本稀有的書很貴，因為不容易找到。

rarely ﹝ˈrɛrlɪ﹞ *adv.* 很少；不常

Mike *rarely* goes to the library because it is very far from his house.

麥克很少去圖書館，因為圖書館離他家很遠。

raspberry
(ˈræzˌbɛrɪ)
n.【植物】覆盆子

The *raspberry* bushes have a lot of fruit this year.
今年覆盆子樹結了許多果實。

rate (ret) n. 速率；速度

The driver reduced his *rate* of speed as he approached the red light.
這名駕駛人在接近紅燈時，將車速減緩。

rather (ˈræðɚ) adv. 相當地

It's *rather* cold today, so I will wear a jacket. 今天相當冷，所以我會穿夾克。

real (ˈriəl) adj. 眞的

Artificial flowers last a long time, but *real* ones do not. 人造花可以持續一段很長的時間，但眞的花卻不行。

reason (ˈrizn̩) n. 原因

The *reason* Hank was late today is that his car broke down. 漢克今天遲到的原因，是因為他的車拋錨了。

recent (ˈrisn̩t) adj. 最近的

I'm looking for a *recent* edition of Time magazine.
我想要找時代雜誌最近的版本。

reception (rɪˈsɛpʃən)
n. 酒會；歡迎會

The wedding ceremony will be held at the church, but the *reception* will be at the Four Seasons hotel.
結婚典禮將在教堂舉行，但喜筵則是在四季飯店舉辦。

reckless (ˈrɛklɪs)
adj. 魯莽的

The *reckless* driver caused a serious accident. 這名魯莽的駕駛人，造成了一起嚴重的車禍。

recognize
(ˈrɛkəɡˌnaɪz) *v.* 認出

Paul has lost so much weight that I almost didn't *recognize* him.
保羅的體重減輕很多，以致於我幾乎認不出他來。

re	+	cognize
again +		*know*

record (ˈrɛkəd) *n.* 紀錄

This is the file where we keep the personnel and medical *records* of every employee.
這個就是我們保存每位員工的人事及**醫療**資料的檔案。

recover (rɪˈkʌvə) *v.*
康復；尋回

If you take this medicine, you will *recover* soon.
如果你把這個藥吃了，你很快就會康復的。

The police were unable to *recover* the stolen goods because they had already been resold.
警方無法找回贓物，因為它們已經被**轉**賣了。

recovery ﹝ rɪˋkʌvərɪ ﹞
n. 康復；取回

Her *recovery* from the flu was very quick; she feels fine now.

她很快地從流行性感冒中康復了；她現在覺得精神很好。

Paul was surprised by the *recovery* of his stolen car; he had thought it was gone for good.

保羅很驚訝能找回他失竊的車；他原以為已經永遠失去它了。

recruit ﹝ rɪˋkrut ﹞ *v.*
招募（新兵）

The military often *recruits* new soldiers right out of high school.

軍方常常從高中應屆畢業生中，招募新兵。

re	+	cruit
again	+	*grow*

redhead ﹝ ˋrɛdˏhɛd ﹞
n. 紅髮的人

Although the Parkers are both blonde, their son is a *redhead*.

雖然帕克斯夫妻兩人都是金髮，他們的兒子卻是紅頭髮。

reenlist ﹝ ˏriɛnˋlɪst ﹞
v. 延長服役時間

Peter has decided not to *reenlist* when his tour of duty is finished. He has had enough of army life.

彼得已經決定在他服兵役期滿後，就不再延長服役時間。他已經受夠了軍隊的生活。

refer (rɪˋfɝ) v. 是指；使求助於

When the professor talked about the importance of being on time, everyone knew that he was *referring* to Bill, who is usually late for class. 當教授談論到準時的重要時，大家都知道，他是在指上課常遲到的比爾。

If the doctor cannot cure your illness himself, he may *refer* you to a specialist. 如果這位醫生自己沒辦法治好你的病，他可能會叫你去找專科醫師。

reference (ˋrɛfərəns) n. 參考

There are a number of *reference* books in the library, such as dictionaries and encyclopedias. 圖書館裡有很多參考書，像是字典和百科全書。

refine (rɪˋfaɪn) v. 精煉

The government approved the new plant that was built to *refine* petroleum. 政府核准建造新的煉油廠。

reflect (rɪˋflɛkt) v. 反射；反映

A mirror will *reflect* your image. 鏡子可以反映出你的影像。

re	+	flect
back	+	bend

reflection (rɪ'flɛkʃən)
n. 影像

The metal is so shiny that I can see my *reflection* in it.
這塊金屬很亮，我可以在上面看到我的影像。

refreshments
(rɪ'frɛʃmənts) *n. pl.* 點心

During the flight, *refreshments* such as soda and juice will be available.
在搭飛機旅行時，可以吃到像汽水和果汁之類的點心。

regardless
(rɪ'gɑrdlɪs) *adv.*
無論如何

Mary will be very late, but I will wait for her, *regardless*.
瑪麗會很晚才到，但無論如何，我都會等她。

region ('ridʒən) *n.* 地區

The desert *region* is dry year round.
沙漠地區一年到頭都是乾燥的。

regret (rɪ'grɛt) *n., v.*
後悔；遺憾

She has no *regret* about turning down his job offer because she doesn't want to move.
她並不後悔拒絕了他所提供的工作，因為她不想搬家。

I *regret* that I cannot attend your party; I will be out of town.
我很遺憾不能參加你的宴會；我將出城去。

regularly ('rɛgjələ‚lɪ)
adv. 定期地;規律地

Helen is in good shape because she exercises *regularly*.
海倫身體很健康;因爲她有定期運動。

regulation
(‚rɛgjə'leʃən) *n.* 規定

There are many *regulations* to follow in the military.
在軍隊裡,有很多規定要遵守。

reject (rɪ'dʒɛkt) *v.*
拒絕;駁回

If your loan application is not complete, the bank will *reject* it.
如果你的貸款申請書不齊全,銀行會加以駁回。

re	+	ject
back	+	*throw*

relate (rɪ'let) *v.* 敘述
v. 有關聯

The reporter asked the survivors to *relate* their experiences in the war.
記者請生還者敘述他們的參戰經驗。

In many sales jobs your income directly *relates* to your performance.
在許多業務方面的工作,收入和工作表現,有直接的關連。

relation (rɪ'leʃən)
n. 關連

The doctor is studying the effects of smoking in *relation* to heart disease.
這名醫生正在研究,吸煙和心臟病之間的關連。

relationship

(rɪˋleʃənˏʃɪp) *n.* 關係

The professor talked about the *relationship* between mass and speed in a moving object. 教授談到了移動中的物體，其質量與速度兩者之間的關係。

relatively (ˋrɛlətɪvlɪ) *adv.* 相當地

Although my suitcase weighs only ten pounds, it is *relatively* heavy compared to yours. 雖然我的手提箱只有十磅重，但跟你的比起來，就顯得相當重。

relaxation

(ˏrilæksˋeʃən) *n.* 娛樂

Although our trip abroad was primarily for business, we still had some time for *relaxation*.
雖然我們的外國之旅主要是為了洽公，但還是有一些時間娛樂。

reliable (rɪˋlaɪəbḷ) *adj.* 耐用的；可靠的

I want to buy a *reliable* car, because I don't want to pay a lot for repairs. 我想買一部耐用的車子，因為我不想付一堆維修費。

relieve (rɪˋliv) *v.* 減輕

The aspirin *relieved* my headache. 阿斯匹靈減輕了我的頭痛。

remote (rɪˋmot) *adj.* 偏僻的；微小的

He is bewildered by the big city because he grew up in a *remote* village. 大城市令他感到很困惑，因為他是在偏僻的村莊長大的。

render 〔'rɛndə 〕*v.*
表示（敬意）

Don't forget to *render* a salute when you meet a superior officer.
當你見到上級長官時，不要忘記敬禮。

repeatedly 〔 rɪ'pitɪdlɪ 〕
adv. 一再地；重覆地

I phoned Tim *repeatedly* last night, but he was not home.
我昨晚一再地打電話給提姆，但是他都不在家。

repel 〔 rɪ'pɛl 〕*v.* 抵擋；
防（水）

The waterproof jacket will *repel* the rain.
這件防水夾克可以防雨。

re	+	pel
back	+	*drive*

replace 〔 rɪ'ples 〕*v.*
更換

This chair is broken and cannot be fixed; we will have to *replace* it.
這把椅子壞了，而且修不好；我們必須換新的。

represent 〔,rɛprɪ'zɛnt 〕
v. 代表；代理

In Morse code, dots and dashes *represent* letters.
在摩斯電碼中，點和線就代表字母。

I will *represent* the chairman at today's meeting.
我將代表主席，參加今天這場會議。

reprimand

(ˈrɛprəˌmænd) *v.* 斥責；
譴責

He was *reprimanded* for coming home too late.

他因為太晚回家，而遭到斥責。

request (rɪˈkwɛst)
v. 要求

This new camera doesn't work; I will *request* a refund.

這台新的相機故障了；我將要求退錢。

The teacher *requests* that we not use our cell phones in class.

老師要求我們，不要在課堂上使用手機。

require (rɪˈkwaɪr)
v. 要求

The school *requires* all students to take PE classes. 這所學校要求所有的
學生，都要上體育課。

```
re   + quire
 |       |
again + seek
```

rescue (ˈrɛskju) *v.* 拯救

Firefighters must often *rescue* people from burning buildings.

消防隊員必須常常從燃燒的建築物中，
將人們救出來。

reserve (rɪˈzɜv) *v.* 預訂

This restaurant is very popular; you should call to *reserve* a table.

這家餐廳非常受歡迎；你應該先打電話
訂位。

```
re   + serve
 |       |
back + keep
```

reservoir ('rɛzə‚vɔr)
n. 水庫

The water level in the ***reservoir*** increased due to the heavy rainfall.
因爲一場豪雨，水庫的水位上升了。

reside (rɪ'zaɪd) *v.* 居住

How long have you ***resided*** here?
你住在這裡多久了？

resident ('rɛzədənt)
n. 居民

Many ***residents*** of Nantou lost their homes in the earthquake. 許多南投的居民，在地震中失去了他們的家。

```
re   + sid + ent
 |      |      |
back + sit  +  n.
```

resign (rɪ'zaɪn) *v.* 辭職

Ian decided to ***resign*** from the bank and open his own business. 艾恩決定辭去銀行的工作，開創他自己的事業。

resist (rɪ'zɪst) *v.* 抗拒；抵擋

Amy ***resisted*** our efforts to help her, insisting that she could do it herself. 艾咪拒絕我們努力幫助她，她堅持自己可以做得到。

The old house could not ***resist*** the strong winds of the typhoon and collapsed. 這棟老房子，禁不起颱風帶來的強風，所以倒塌了。

```
re    + sist
 |       |
against + stand
```

resistance ﹝ rɪˈzɪstəns ﹞
n. 反抗

The principal met a great deal of *resistance* when he asked the teachers to work on Sunday.

當校長要求老師們在星期日上班時，遭遇了許多反抗。

resource ﹝ rɪˈsors ﹞
n. 資源

Water is an important *resource* in desert areas.

水在沙漠地區是重要的資源。

respect ﹝ rɪˈspɛkt ﹞ n.
敬意；尊敬

The Japanese often show their *respect* by bowing. 日本人常以鞠躬表示敬意。

re	+	spect
again	+	*see*

respiratory
﹝ rɪˈspaɪrəˌtorɪ ﹞ adj.
呼吸系統的

After hearing the patient's cough, the doctor diagnosed a *respiratory* illness. 醫生在聽了這位病人的咳嗽聲後，診斷爲呼吸系統的疾病。

re	+	spira	+	tory
back	+	*breathe*	+	*adj.*

responsibility
﹝ rɪˌspɑnsəˈbɪlətɪ ﹞ n.
責任；義務

Washing the dishes is one of the girl's daily *responsibilities*.

洗這些盤子，是這個女孩每天的責任之一。

responsible
(rɪ'spɑnsəbḷ) *adj.*
負責任的

A *responsible* person does what he is supposed to do.
一個負責任的人，會做他應該做的事。

result (rɪ'zʌlt) *v.* 引起

Heavy rains often *result* in flooding.
豪雨常會引起水災。

retain (rɪ'ten) *v.* 保留

A dam was built to *retain* water in the lake.
水壩是建來把水留在湖裡的。

```
re   + tain
 |      |
back + hold
```

retired (rɪ'taɪrd) *adj.*
退休的

My father is *retired* now so he no longer has to commute to his office.
我爸爸現在已經退休了，所以他不再需要通勤到公司了。

retirement
(rɪ'taɪrmənt) *n.* 退休

The lawyer took an early *retirement*; he was only 50 when he stopped working. 這位律師提早退休了；他五十歲就停止工作了。

retreat (rɪ'trit) *v.* 撤退

When the commander realized he could not win the battle he gave the order to *retreat*. 當這位指揮官了解到他無法打贏這場戰爭時，他下令撤退。

```
re   + treat
 |      |
back + draw
```

reveal ﹝ rɪ'vil ﹞ *v.* 透露

The reporter insisted that he could not *reveal* his sources.
這名記者堅持不透露他的消息來源。

```
 re   + veal
  |       |
back + veil (取下面紗)
```

reverse ﹝ rɪ'vɜs ﹞ *n.*
後退；倒轉

Ted put the car into *reverse* and backed out of the parking space.
泰德將車倒退，駛出停車位。

revolve ﹝ rɪ'vɑlv ﹞ *v.*
旋轉

Centuries ago people believed that the universe *revolved* around the Earth. 幾世紀以前，人們相信宇宙是繞著地球旋轉的。

ride ﹝ raɪd ﹞ *n.* 搭乘

My sister gave me a *ride* to work today. 今天我姊姊載我去上班。

right ﹝ raɪt ﹞ *n.* 權利

Only members of the club have the *right* to enter.
只有俱樂部的會員，才有權利進入。

rigid ﹝ 'rɪdʒɪd ﹞ *adj.*
堅硬的

The box is made of a *rigid* material and is very strong.
這個箱子是用很堅硬的材料做成的，非常堅固。

risk 〔rɪsk〕*v.* 冒險

Don't *risk* your life by driving a motorcycle without a helmet.
不要冒生命危險，騎車不戴安全帽。

rivet 〔'rɪvɪt〕*n.* 鉚丁

This metal desk is held together with *rivets*.
這張金屬製的書桌，是用鉚丁接合的。

rocket 〔'rɑkɪt〕*n.*
火箭武器（炸彈、飛彈等）

The plane was shot down by a *rocket*.
這架飛機被一枚飛彈擊落。

rod 〔rɑd〕*n.* 桿；竿

We hung the curtains from a *rod* over the window.
我們將窗簾掛在竿子上，垂落在窗戶上。

roll 〔rol〕*v.* 行駛；翻滾

The driver forgot to put on the emergency brake and the car *rolled* down the hill. 這名駕駛人忘記踩緊急煞車，於是車子駛下了山坡。

The patient required the help of the nurse to *roll* over in bed.
這名病人需要護士的幫忙，才能在床上翻身。

rotary 〔'rotərɪ〕*adj.*
旋轉的

The *rotary* movement of the fan's blades is what creates a flow of air.
電風扇扇葉的旋轉動作，能製造氣流。

rotate 〔'rotet 〕*v.* 旋轉

A CD *rotates* at high speed when you play it.

當你播放 CD 時，它會以高速旋轉。

rotor 〔'rotɚ 〕*n.* （直升機的）旋轉翼

One of the *rotors* is damaged so the helicopter cannot fly.

這架直昇機不能飛行，因為其中一個旋轉翼壞了。

rough 〔 rʌf 〕*adj.* 粗糙的

This material feels very *rough* against my skin; I would prefer something smoother.

我覺得這種質料很粗糙；我比較喜歡較平滑的。

routine 〔 ru'tin 〕*adj.* 例行的　*n.* 例行公事

The doctor assured me that it was a *routine* operation, one that he had performed many times.

醫生向我保證，這只是例行的手術，他已經進行過很多次了。

Reading the newspaper is part of his daily *routine*.

看報紙是他每天的例行公事的一部份。

row 〔 ro 〕*n.* 排

I don't like to sit in the first *row* because it is difficult to see the screen.

我不喜歡坐在第一排，因為很難看到銀幕。

runway (ˋrʌn͵we) *n.* 跑道	The pilot was told to take off from *runway* number two. 飛行員被通知，必須從二號跑道起飛。
rush (rʌʃ) *n.* 匆忙； 蜂擁的人群　*v.* 匆忙	There was a great *rush* to get on the bus. 有一大群人擠著想上公車。 If you get up earlier, you won't have to *rush* to work. 如果你早點起床，就不必趕著去上班。
rust (rʌst) *n.* 銹	The old car has a great deal of *rust* on it. 那輛舊車上面，生了很多銹。

【劉毅老師的話】

　　「比較法」是背單字的好方法。如：
runway（跑道）不認識，先背 run（跑），
再加上 way（道路），就容易多了。rush
（匆忙）背不下來，就先背 brush（刷子）。
儘量用已會的單字，背不會的單字。

S

safety (ˈseftɪ) *n.* 安全

The captain is required to provide enough life jackets for all passengers in order to guarantee their *safety*.

為了保障所有乘客的安全，機長被要求，要提供足夠的救生衣給所有乘客。

sail (sel) *v.* 航行

The ship will *sail* at noon tomorrow.

這艘船明天中午啟航。

salary (ˈsælərɪ) *n.* 薪水

He is looking for a job with a higher *salary* because he finds it difficult to live on the money he makes now.

他在找一個薪水較高的工作，因為他覺得要靠現在所賺的錢過活是很困難的。

salute (səˈlut) *v.* 向…敬禮

The soldiers *saluted* the colonel as he walked by.

軍人們在上校經過時敬禮。

sand (sænd) *v.* 用砂紙磨

The carpenter must *sand* the table before it is painted.

木匠在為這張桌子油漆之前，必須先用砂紙磨過。

sandpaper
('sænd,pepɚ) *n.* 砂紙

We can use *sandpaper* to make this old wood smooth.

我們可以用砂紙，讓這塊古老的木頭變得平滑。

satellite ('sætḷ,aɪt) *n.*
衛星

Communication has been improved by the use of *satellites*.

通訊狀況因為使用衛星而獲得改善。

satisfactory
(,sætɪs'fæktrɪ) *adj.*
令人滿意的

His boss said that his job performance was *satisfactory*.

他的老闆說，他的工作表現令人滿意。

saturate ('sætʃə,ret)
v. 使溼透

When water *saturates* the towel, the towel becomes very heavy.

當水使毛巾溼透時，毛巾會變得很重。

sauce (sɔs) *n.*
醬；醬汁

Would you like some chocolate *sauce* on your ice cream?

你的冰淇淋要不要加一些巧克力醬？

scarcely ('skɛrslɪ)
adv. 幾乎不

The hikers were so tired after their long walk that they could *scarcely* move.

這些徒步旅行者在長途跋涉後非常疲倦，幾乎都快走不動了。

scared〔skɛrd〕*adj.*
受驚嚇的

The dog was *scared* by the loud thunder and hid under the bed.
這隻狗被巨大的雷聲嚇到，躲到床底下去了。

scary〔ˈskɛrɪ〕*adj.*
恐怖的

The children cried during the *scary* movie.
這些小孩在看恐怖電影的時候哭了。

scatter〔ˈskætɚ〕*v.*
散播

The farmer *scattered* the corn on the ground and the hens began to eat.
農夫將穀粒灑在地上，然後母雞就開始啄食。

scenery〔ˈsinərɪ〕*n.*
風景

The mountain *scenery* was beautiful and we took many pictures of it.
這座山的風景非常美麗，我們拍了許多照片。

scientific〔ˌsaɪənˈtɪfɪk〕
adj. 科學的

This university has strong programs in all the *scientific* fields, including chemistry and physics.
這所大學在科學領域方面的所有課程都很強，包括化學和物理。

scissors〔ˈsɪzɚz〕
n. pl. 剪刀

You may use my *scissors* to cut that paper. 你可以用我的剪刀來剪那張紙。

scope (skop) *n.* 範圍

The low-flying plane was under the *scope* of the radar.
這架低空飛行的飛機，位在雷達偵測的範圍之下。

scream (skrim) *v.* 尖叫

My mother *screamed* when she saw the stranger at the window.　當我媽媽看到窗外有陌生人時，她大聲尖叫。

screen (skrin) *n.* 螢幕

If you look at the computer *screen* for too long, your eyes will become tired.　如果你盯著電腦螢幕太久，你的眼睛會變得疲倦。

screw (skru) *n.* 螺絲釘

We had to assemble the table ourselves, but all the *screws* and other hardware were included.
我們必須自己裝配桌子，不過所有的螺絲和其他的金屬器件都包括在內了。

screwdriver ('skru,draɪvɚ) *n.* 螺絲起子

You will need a *screwdriver* to unscrew that panel.
你需要一個螺絲起子，來旋開儀表盤。

scrub (skrʌb) *v.* 刷洗

The soldiers were ordered to *scrub* the floor of the barracks in preparation for the inspection.
士兵們被命令刷洗營房的地板，以備檢查。

seal ﹝ sil ﹞ *v.* 密封

The package was *sealed* with tape.
這個包裹是用膠帶密封的。

seaman ﹝'simən ﹞ *n.*
水兵

In the navy, the *seamen* must obey the orders of the captain.
在海軍裡，水兵們必須服從船長的命令。

seaport ﹝'si͵port ﹞ *n.*
海港

The busy *seaport* is always filled with ships from around the world.
這個熱鬧的海港總是充滿了從世界各地來的船。

search ﹝ sɝtʃ ﹞ *v.* 搜查

The police officers *searched* the suspect's house for evidence.
警方在嫌犯的家中搜查證據。

secondary
﹝'sɛkənd͵ɛrɪ ﹞ *adj.* 第二的

The comfort of the airplane is a *secondary* concern; the most important issue is whether or not it is safe.
飛機的舒適度是第二考量；最重要的問題在於是否安全。

section ﹝'sɛkʃən ﹞ *n.*
部分

This *section* of the highway is under repair and drivers are asked to take a detour around it.
這段公路正在修復中，駕駛人被要求繞道行駛。

security 〔 sɪ'kjurətɪ 〕
adj. 安全的　*n.* 安全

Dave is working as a private *security* guard at the warehouse.
戴夫在倉庫擔任私人警衛。

seem 〔 sim 〕 *v.* 似乎

You *seem* to have a fever; we had better check your temperature with a thermometer. 你似乎發燒了；我們最好用溫度計檢查一下你的體溫。

segment 〔 'sɛgmənt 〕
n. 部分

Our team was ahead until the last *segment* of the relay race.
我們這一隊一直到接力賽的最後一棒，都保持領先。

self-confidence
〔 'sɛlf'kɑnfədəns 〕 *n.* 自信

Peter has a lot of *self-confidence* and never doubts that he can do something well. 彼得很有自信，且從未懷疑自己是否能將某件事做好。

selfish 〔 'sɛlfɪʃ 〕 *adj.*
自私的

The children are very *selfish* and don't like to share their toys.
孩子們都非常自私，不喜歡和別人分享他們的玩具。

senior 〔 'sinjɚ 〕 *adj.*
地位較高的；資深的

In the military you must salute an officer who is *senior* to you in rank.
在軍隊中，你必須向官階比你高的長官敬禮。

seniority 〔 sin'jɔrətɪ 〕
n. 資深;地位高

A colonel has *seniority* over a
lieutenant. 上校的地位高於上尉。

sense 〔 sɛns 〕 *n.* 感覺

His *sense* of duty did not allow him
to leave until the work was complete.
他的責任感,不容許他在工作完成之前
離開。

sensible 〔'sɛnsəbḷ 〕
adj. 明智的

It is *sensible* to bring an umbrella
because it may rain.
帶雨傘是明智的做法,因為可能會下雨。

sequence 〔'sikwəns 〕
n. 順序

These files are out of *sequence*; please
put them in order. 這些檔案的順序亂
了;請把它們按順序排列。

sergeant 〔'sɑrdʒənt 〕
n. 中士

The *sergeant* ordered his men to
report for duty at 6:00.
中士要求他的部下,在六點時報到上班。

series 〔'sɪrɪz 〕 *n.*
影集;系列

I missed the first episode of the TV
series, so it is difficult for me to
understand the story.
我錯過了這部影集的第一集,所以我覺得,
要了解故事情節並不容易。

serve 〔 sɝv 〕 *v.*
服役;服務

He has *served* in the military for nearly
20 years. 他待在軍隊服役將近二十年了。

service ('sɜvɪs) *n.*
（海、陸、空）軍；兵役

Frank wanted to join the *service* after high school so he paid a visit to the army recruiting office.

法蘭克高中畢業後想從軍，所以他去參觀軍隊的徵兵處。

set (sɛt) *v.* 放置

Please *set* the vase down carefully; it is very fragile.

請小心放下這只花瓶；它十分易碎。

sex (sɛks) *n.* 性別

Applicants of either *sex* may apply for the position.

應徵者不分男女，都可以應徵這份工作。

shallow ('ʃælo) *adj.*
淺的

The swimming pool is too *shallow* to dive into.

這個游泳池太淺了，沒辦法潛水。

shape (ʃep) *v.*
將…塑造成某個形狀

The artist *shaped* the clay into the form of a lion.

這位藝術家將黏土塑成獅子的形狀。

shatter ('ʃætɚ) *v.*
使粉碎

The explosion *shattered* the windows of the shop. 爆炸使這家店的窗戶都碎了。

shell (ʃɛl) *n.* 彈殼

After the shooting, the police collected the empty *shells* as evidence.

射擊之後，警方收集了空彈殼作爲證據。

shield 〔 ʃild 〕 *n.* 遮蔽物

The beach umbrella acts as a *shield* against the strong sun.

海灘傘可作爲預防烈日的遮蔽物。

shock 〔 ʃɑk 〕 *n.* 電擊；觸電

The electrician received a *shock* when he touched the bare wire.

那名電工在接觸裸露的電線時觸電了。

shot 〔 ʃɑt 〕 *n.* 注射

The doctor gave me a *shot* and told me to rest until I felt better.

醫生幫我打了一針，然後要我好好休息，直到身體恢復爲止。

shout 〔 ʃaʊt 〕 *v.* 大叫

You are not allowed to *shout* in the library. 你不能在圖書館裡大吼大叫。

shovel 〔 'ʃʌvl̩ 〕 *n.* 鏟子

The workmen used *shovels* to dig the hole.

工人用鏟子挖了一個洞。

sight 〔 saɪt 〕 *n.* 視力

The old man said his *sight* was not as good as it used to be.

這位老先生說他的視力不如從前了。

silent 〔 'saɪlənt 〕 *adj.* 安靜的

The teacher asked us to be *silent* during the exam.

老師要求我們，考試時要保持安靜。

silo〔'saɪlo〕 *n.* 筒倉
（貯存糧食的圓柱形倉庫）

The farmer stored the wheat in the *silo*.
農夫將小麥儲存在筒倉裡。

similarly〔'sɪmələˈlɪ〕
adv. 同樣地

The twins not only look alike, but also
behave *similarly*.
這對雙胞胎不但長得很像，而且行為舉止也
一樣。

simple〔'sɪmpḷ〕*adj.*
簡單的

The problem was very *simple* and we
solved it quickly.
這個問題很簡單，我們很快就解決了。

sing〔sɪŋ〕*v.* 唱（歌）

It is customary to *sing* "Happy Birthday"
to someone who is celebrating his
birthday.　我們習慣在有人慶祝生日時，
唱「生日快樂歌」。

site〔saɪt〕*n.* 地點；
用地

The empty field has been chosen as the
site of the stadium.
這片空地已被選為體育館用地。

skeleton〔'skɛlətṇ〕
n. 骨骼

The X-ray gave the doctor a clear
picture of the patient's *skeleton*.
X光片讓醫生能清楚地看見病人的骨骼。

skill〔skɪl〕*n.* 技巧；
技術

The winning marksman showed his
skill in the shooting contest.
優勝的射手在射擊比賽中，展現他的技巧。

skilled〔skɪld〕*adj.*
有技巧的;熟練的

Kim is a *skilled* tennis player and has won many championships.
金姆是個技巧高超的網球選手,贏得了許多冠軍。

skip〔skɪp〕*v.* 略過;
跳過

Harry had to *skip* his morning jog because he overslept.
哈利必須略過晨跑,因為他睡過頭了。

skull〔skʌl〕*n.* 頭顱

Wearing a helmet will protect your *skull* in the event of an accident.
戴安全帽,可以在發生車禍時,保護你的頭部。

slam〔slæm〕*v.*
砰然關閉(門、窗等)

Please don't *slam* the door; shut it gently.
請不要砰然把門關上;要輕輕地關門。

sleep〔slip〕*n.* 睡眠
v. 睡覺

It is important to get enough *sleep* if you want to maintain good health.
如果你要保持良好的健康,充足的睡眠是很重要的。

slice〔slaɪs〕*v.* 切
n. 薄片

I am going to *slice* the cake. Do you want a big piece or a small piece?
我要切蛋糕了。你要大塊的還是小塊的?

slide 〔 slaɪd 〕 *v.* 滑動

In order to use the computer mouse, you must *slide* it over a smooth surface.
要使用電腦滑鼠，你必須讓滑鼠在平坦的表面上滑動。

slight 〔 slaɪt 〕 *adj.*
輕微的

The leaves of the tree move gently in the *slight* breeze.
樹葉在微風中輕柔地飄動。

smart 〔 smɑrt 〕 *adj.*
聰明的

It is obvious he is a *smart* boy because he can read at the age of three.
顯然他是一個聰明的男孩，因為他三歲時就會閱讀了。

smell 〔 smɛl 〕 *n.*
氣味；香味

As they passed the bakery, the passersby were tempted by the *smell* of freshly baked bread.
路過麵包店的行人，都被剛出爐的麵包香味所引誘。

smooth 〔 smuð 〕 *adj.*
平滑的

The carpenter sanded the rough wood until it was *smooth*. 木匠用砂紙磨這塊粗糙的木頭，直到它變得平滑為止。

smoothly 〔'smuðlɪ〕
adv. 順利地

Thanks to the committee's careful planning, the ceremony went *smoothly*.
多虧委員會的細心策劃，典禮進行得很順利。

snake 〔 snek 〕 *n.* 蛇

Snakes prefer a warm climate because they are cold-blooded animals.

蛇比較喜歡溫暖的氣候，因為牠們是冷血動物。

soak 〔 sok 〕 *v.* 浸泡；弄濕

The clothing left outside was *soaked* by the rain.

留在外面的衣服，被雨淋濕了。

soft 〔 sɔft 〕 *adj.* （聲音）柔和的；低的；輕的

It is sometimes difficult to hear Tom because he has a *soft* voice.

有時候很難聽清楚湯姆說的話，因為他的聲音很低。

softly 〔'sɔftlɪ 〕 *adv.* 低聲地

The teacher asked us to speak *softly* in the library.

老師要求我們，在圖書館裡要低聲說話。

soil 〔 sɔɪl 〕 *n.* 土壤

The *soil* here is very rich, so the farmers always have a good harvest.

這裡的土壤很肥沃，所以農夫們的收成一向很好。

solder 〔'sadɚ 〕 *v.* 焊接

These two pieces of metal will have to be *soldered* together.

這兩塊金屬得焊接在一起。

solid ('salıd) *adj.* 固體的

Many materials can exist in either a *solid* or liquid state, for example, water. 許多物質能以固體或液體的狀態存在，例如水。

solidify (sə'lıdə,faı) *v.* 凝固

When water freezes it *solidifies*. 水結冰時會凝固。

somewhat ('sʌm,hwɑt) *adv.* 有點

We were *somewhat* tired after the long hike. 在長途健行後，我們有點累。

sonar ('sonɑr) *n.* 聲納

A submarine uses *sonar* to navigate through the water. 潛水艇利用聲納在水中航行。

sort (sɔrt) *n.* 種類

This *sort* of jacket is in fashion now. 這種夾克現在正流行。

source (sors) *n.* 來源

The *source* of this spring is in the mountains. 這股泉水的源頭在山裡。

space (spes) *n.* 空間；太空

There is not enough *space* in the auditorium for 300 seats. 禮堂沒有足夠的空間，容納三百個座位。

People have long dreamed of traveling through *space* to another planet. 人們長久以來都夢想著，要穿越太空到其他行星旅行。

specific ﹝ spɪˋsɪfɪk ﹞
adj. 明確的

Please tell me the *specific* details of your plan.
請告訴我，你的計劃的明確細節。

specify ﹝ˋspɛsəˌfaɪ﹞
v. 明確指出

Please ask the mechanic to *specify* what kind of repairs he will make to the car. 請要求技工明確指出，他將對這輛車進行哪一種維修的工作。

```
spec  +  ify
 |        |
see   +  make
```

spin ﹝ spɪn ﹞ *v.* 使旋轉

You can do tricks with a yo-yo by *spinning* it.
你可以旋轉溜溜球，來表演特技。

spine ﹝ spaɪn ﹞ *n.* 脊椎骨

The driver injured his *spine* in the accident and had to have back surgery. 這位駕駛人的脊椎骨在車禍中受傷了，必須動背部手術。

splice ﹝ splaɪs ﹞ *v.* 接合

The electrician *spliced* the two wires together. 電工將兩條電線接在一起。

spot ﹝ spat ﹞ *v.*
發現；找出

The fisherman looked through his binoculars, trying to *spot* the island.
漁夫透過他的雙筒望遠鏡，試著找出這座島。

spouse 〔 spaʊz 〕 *n.*
配偶

John came to the party, but his *spouse* stayed at home with their children.

約翰去參加宴會，而他的太太留在家裡陪孩子。

sprained 〔 sprend 〕
adj. 扭傷的

The doctor told me I had a *sprained* ankle and suggested that I walk as little as possible.

醫生說我的腳踝扭傷了，並建議我儘量少走路。

spread 〔 sprɛd 〕 *v.*
傳播；舖（桌布）

John *spread* the news of the surprise party to all of Kathy's friends.

約翰向凱西所有的朋友傳達，將舉辦驚喜宴會的消息。

The table was *spread* with a white cloth for the special dinner. 爲了這頓特別的晚餐，桌上舖了白色的桌布。

squad 〔 swɑd 〕 *n.*
小隊；小組

The *squad* was ordered to report for duty immediately.

這個小組接獲命令，要立刻報到上班。

squeeze 〔 skwiz 〕 *v.*
擠壓

Please don't *squeeze* the fruit; you might bruise it.

請不要擠壓水果；你可能會碰傷它。

stable ('stebḷ) *adj.* 穩定的

The weather has been *stable* recently, but a storm is predicted for tomorrow.
最近天氣一直很穩定,但是預報指出,明天會有暴風雨。

stack (stæk) *n.* 堆
v. 堆放;堆積

There is a *stack* of books on the table.
桌上有一堆書。

The waiter *stacked* the clean plates neatly on the shelf.
服務生將乾淨的盤子,整齊地堆放在架子上。

staff (stæf) *n.* 全體職員 (集合名詞)

The manager decided to give his *staff* the day off as a reward for their hard work. 經理決定要放員工一天假,以作爲他們努力工作的獎賞。

stage (stedʒ) *n.* 舞台

It was impossible to see the *stage* from the back of the theater.
從劇場的後方,不可能看得到舞台。

stale (stel) *adj.* 不新鮮的

We can't eat this bread because it is *stale*. 我們不能吃這個麵包,因爲它不新鮮。

stand (stænd) *v.* 忍受

Would you mind if I changed the radio station? I can't *stand* this kind of music. 你介意我換個廣播電台嗎?我無法忍受這種音樂。

starboard ('star,bɔrd)
adj. 右舷的

The seaman was told to start mopping the deck on the *starboard* side.

船員被告知，要開始用拖把拖右舷那一側的甲板。

starve (starv) *v.* 飢餓

Because we did not have time to eat breakfast, we were *starving* by noon.

因為沒時間吃早餐，所以我們中午的時候就餓了。

static ('stætɪk) *n.*
電波干擾

There is so much *static* that I can't hear this radio station clearly.

有太多電波干擾，以致於我無法清楚地聽見這個電台的廣播。

station ('steʃən) *n.*
【軍事】駐地；基地

After completing basic training, the recruit learned that his duty *station* would be overseas.

在完成基本訓練之後，這位新兵得知，他的工作基地將會是在海外。

stationary
('steʃən,ɛrɪ) *adj.* 固定的

He likes to exercise by riding a *stationary* bicycle while watching TV. 他喜歡在看電視時，騎在固定的腳踏車上運動。

sta	+ tion	+ ary
stand +	*n.* +	*adj.*

steady ('stɛdɪ) *adj.*
穩定的;固定的

We made *steady* progress on the task of painting the room.
我們油漆房間的工作,有穩定的進展。

There have been a *steady* number of immigrants entering the country each year. 這個國家,每年都有固定數量的移民移入。

steak (stek) *n.* 牛排

We like to cook our *steaks* on the barbecue outside.
我們喜歡把牛排拿到外面的烤肉架上烤。

steal (stil) *v.* 偷

He swears that he did not *steal* the money, but we suspect that he is indeed the thief.
他發誓說他沒有偷錢,但我們懷疑他的確是小偷。

steam (stim) *n.* 蒸氣

The water is so hot that we can see *steam* rising from it.
水非常熱,以致於我們可以看到蒸氣從裡面冒出來。

steel (stil) *n.* 鋼鐵

The old wooden bridge was replaced with a strong one made of *steel*.
那座老木橋,被鋼鐵製的堅固橋樑所取代。

steer (stɪr) *v.*
操縱；駕駛

Without his glasses, Jim could not *steer* the car well and he hit a tree.
吉姆沒戴眼鏡，就沒辦法好好開車，而且他還撞到樹。

step (stɛp) *n.* 步驟

Filling out the application form is merely the first *step* in seeking admission to the college. You must also take an entrance exam and attend an interview.
填寫申請表，只是獲得入學許可的第一步。你還必須參加入學考試和面試。

stern (stɜn) *n.* 船尾

We were fishing from the *stern* of the boat. 我們從船尾釣魚。

stingy ('stɪndʒɪ) *adj.*
吝嗇的；小氣的

Although he is a wealthy man, he is *stingy* with his money and would rather keep it in the bank than spend it.
雖然他是個有錢人，但他花錢很小氣，寧願把錢存在銀行，也不願意花掉。

stock (stɑk) *n.* 存貨

We have several of the blue shirts in *stock*, but we are out of the black ones.
我們庫存還有幾件藍色襯衫，但黑色的已經沒有了。

storage (ˈstorɪdʒ) *n.*
保管;倉庫

Proper *storage* of the sports equipment is the responsibility of the PE teacher.
適當地保管運動器材,是體育老師的責任。

store (stor) *v.* 儲存

We *store* a lot of things that we seldom use in the attic.
我們將許多很少用到的東西,放在閣樓裡。

strange (strendʒ)
adj. 奇怪的

The campers saw a *strange* sight in the sky and thought it was a UFO.
露營者看到空中有奇怪的景象,並認為那是幽浮。

strawberry
(ˈstrɔ͵bɛrɪ) *n.* 草莓

She prefers *strawberry* ice cream to chocolate. 她喜歡草莓口味的冰淇淋,甚於巧克力口味的。

stress (strɛs) *v.* 強調
n. 壓力

My doctor *stressed* the fact that smoking is bad for my health.
我的醫生跟我強調,吸煙有害健康的事實。

stretch (strɛtʃ) *v.*
伸出;延伸;拉長

The catcher *stretched* out his arm to catch the ball. 捕手伸出他的手臂去接球。

This road *stretches* from Taipei to Kaohsiung. 這條路從台北延伸到高雄。

He *stretched* the rubber band too far and it broke.
他把橡皮圈拉得太遠,所以它就斷了。

strict 〔 strɪkt 〕 *adj.*
嚴格的

The company has very *strict* rules about giving information to outsiders.
公司對於把情報洩漏給外人，有非常**嚴格**的規定。

strip 〔 strɪp 〕 *n.*
細長的一條

I used *strips* of tape to attach the poster to the wall.
我用細長的膠帶，把海報黏在牆上。

structure 〔 'strʌktʃə 〕
n. 建築物

The building will be preserved because it is a historic *structure*.
這棟建築物將被保存下來，因為它是個具有歷史性的建築。

stuff 〔 stʌf 〕 *n.* 東西

I need a bigger suitcase; I can't fit all this *stuff* in here.
我需要一個大一點的皮箱；我沒辦法將所有的東西塞進這裡。

stupid 〔 'stjupɪd 〕 *adj.*
愚蠢的

Leaving the door unlocked when you went out was a *stupid* thing to do.
外出時不將門上鎖，是一件愚蠢的事。

style 〔 staɪl 〕 *n.* 款式；
方式

This suitcase comes in two *styles*.
這個手提箱有兩種款式。

We were all impressed by his *style* of speaking.
他說話的方式，使我們印象深刻。

submarine

(,sʌbməˈrin) *n.* 潛水艇

The *submarine* was involved in a survey of the ocean floor.

這艘潛水艇加入了勘查海底的行動。

```
sub  + marine
 |        |
under +  sea
```

submerge (səbˈmɝdʒ)
v. 沉入水中

The submarine captain gave the order to *submerge*.

這艘潛水艇的船長，下令沉入水中。

subordinate

(səˈbɔrdn̩ɪt) *n.* 部屬

The soldiers are happy to serve under Colonel Watson because he always treats his *subordinates* fairly.

士兵們很高興爲瓦特森上校效勞，因爲他總是公平地對待部屬。

subscribe

(səbˈskraɪb) *v.*
訂閱 < *to* >

I like the magazine so much that I decided to *subscribe* to it.

我非常喜歡這本雜誌，所以我決定要訂閱它。

```
sub  + scribe
 |       |
under + write
```

substance (ˈsʌbstəns)
n. 物質

The powder is composed of a poisonous *substance* so be careful not to touch it.

這粉末是由一種有毒的物質構成，所以小心不要碰到它。

substitute 〔'sʌbstəˌtjut 〕
v. 代替

substitute A *for* B
用 A 代替 B

I'll have a number three meal, but I'd like to *substitute* a small orange juice for the Coke.
我要一份三號餐，但我想把可口可樂換成小杯柳橙汁。

successful 〔 sək'sɛsfəl 〕
adj. 成功的

The experiment was *successful* and it proved the scientist's hypothesis.
實驗成功了，而且也證明了這位科學家的假設。

sufficient 〔 sə'fɪʃənt 〕
adj. 足夠的

The number of desks is not *sufficient* to accommodate all of the students.
書桌的數量，不夠容納所有的學生。

suggest 〔 sə'dʒɛst 〕 *v.*
建議

I *suggest* that we put off the activity until the weather clears up.
我建議我們將活動，延期到天氣轉好再辦。

support 〔 sə'port 〕 *v.*
支持

The committee took a vote and it was found that most members *supported* the plan.
委員會舉行了投票，發現大多數的會員都支持這項計劃。

```
sup  +  port
 |       |
 up  +  carry
```

surge〔 sɝdʒ 〕 v.
蜂擁而至；急劇上升

The crowd *surged* toward the exits when someone shouted, "Fire!" 當有人大叫「失火了！」時，群眾都湧向出口。

The price of vegetables will *surge* after a typhoon. 蔬菜價格在颱風過後會暴漲。

surgeon〔 'sɝdʒən 〕 n.
外科醫生；軍醫

The *surgeon* was called to the hospital for an emergency operation in the middle of the night. 這名外科醫生在半夜被召回醫院，進行緊急手術。

surgery〔 'sɝdʒɪrɪ 〕 n.
手術

Since it was a minor operation, the *surgery* took less than one hour.
因為是一場小手術，所以不到一小時就完成了。

surprise〔 sə'praɪz 〕
n. 驚訝；令人驚訝的事

The birthday party was a *surprise* to Mary because everyone had kept the secret well.
這場生日宴會使瑪麗十分驚訝，因為大家都把這個秘密保守得很好。

surrender
〔 sə'rɛndɚ 〕 v. 投降

The sergeant ordered the enemy soldiers to put down their weapons and *surrender*. 中士命令敵軍放下武器投降。

sur	+ render
upon	+ give

surround (sə'raund)
v. 圍繞；環繞

The island is *surrounded* by water.
這座島被水環繞。

```
sur + round
 |      |
over + round
```

surroundings
(sə'raundıŋz) *n. pl.* 環境

We were not happy with our
surroundings, so we decided to move.
我們不滿意周圍環境，所以決定要搬家。

survive (sə'vaɪv) *v.*
生還；自…中生還

Only three of the passengers
survived the crash.
只有三位乘客從墜機事件中生還。

suspend (sə'spɛnd)
v. 懸吊

We can *suspend* the children's swing
from this tree branch.
我們可以將孩子們的鞦
韆，掛在這個樹枝上。

```
sus  + pend
 |       |
under + hang
```

sustain (sə'sten) *v.*
維持；支撐

When running a long race, you should
go slowly at first, because it is
difficult to *sustain* a fast pace for
a long time.
當參加長跑比賽時，你剛開始必須慢慢
跑，因為要長時間維持很快的速度是很
困難的。

```
sus + tain
 |      |
up  + keep
```

swallow 〔'swɑlo 〕 *v.*
吞下

It is difficult to *swallow* these pills
because they are so large.
要吞下這些藥丸是很困難的，因爲它們太
大顆了。

switch 〔 swɪtʃ 〕 *n.* 開關

I had difficulty finding the light
switch in the dark.
我很難在黑暗中找到電燈開關。

symbol 〔'sɪmbḷ 〕 *n.* 象徵

Around the world, a white dove is
a *symbol* of peace.
在全世界，白鴿是和平的象徵。

symphony 〔'sɪmfənɪ 〕
n. 交響樂團

Julie is excited about going to the
symphony because she enjoys
classical music.
茱麗對於要去聽交響樂團演奏覺得很
興奮，因爲她很喜歡古典音樂。

sym	+ phony
together	+ *sound*

systematic
〔ˌsɪstə'mætɪk 〕 *adj.*
有系統的

We must conduct the experiment in
a *systematic* way so as to reduce the
chance of careless errors.
我們必須有系統地做這個實驗，以便減少
粗心犯錯的機會。

T

tail (tel) *n.* 尾巴；機尾

The cat meowed loudly when I stepped on its *tail*. 當我踩到這隻貓的尾巴時，牠大聲地喵喵叫。

The plane suffered a great deal of damage in the crash, but the *tail* is still intact. 這架飛機在墜毀時受到嚴重損壞，但機尾的部分卻仍然十分完整。

tank (tæŋk) *n.* 坦克車

The general ordered the *tanks* to roll into town. 將軍命令坦克車開入城裡。

target ('tɑrgɪt) *n.* 靶；目標

The recruit received a good score in marksmanship because he hit the *target* every time.
這名新兵在射擊項目得高分，因為他每次都命中目標。

taste (test) *n.* 味道

The *taste* of this dish is unusual; it's both sweet and spicy.
這道菜的味道很獨特；它是又甜又辣的。

teamwork ('tim,wʒk) *n.* 團隊合作

This job will require *teamwork*; none of us could do it alone.
這個工作需要團隊合作；我們沒有人可以獨力完成。

technician 〔 tɛk'nɪʃən 〕
n. 技術人員

The medical *technician* took an X-ray of the paitent's leg.

這位醫學技術人員，替病人的腿部拍了一張 X 光片。

techn +	ic	+ ian
skill +	carry +	n.

technique 〔 tɛk'nik 〕
n. 技巧；技術

We were all impressed by the pitcher's *technique* when he threw the ball.

我們都對那名投手投球時的技巧印象深刻。

technology
〔 tɛk'nɑlədʒɪ 〕 *n.* 科技

With the help of *technology*, it is now faster and easier to communicate with people around the world.

由於科技的幫助，現在我們能更快而且更容易地，和世界各地的人們聯繫。

telegram 〔'tɛlə,græm 〕
n. 電報

The urgent news was sent by *telegram*. 緊急消息是以發電報來傳遞。

tele +	gram
far off +	write

temporary
〔'tɛmpə,rɛrɪ 〕 *adj.* 暫時
的；臨時的

Unable to find a permanent job, he took a *temporary* position as a clerk.

他找不到永久的工作，於是就暫時先擔任店員這個職務。

tend〔tɛnd〕*v.* 易於

The car *tends* to stall in hot weather.
車子在炎熱的天氣裡容易拋錨。

tendency〔'tɛndənsɪ〕
n. 傾向

He has a *tendency* to leave things
until the last minute.
他有把事情留到最後一分鐘的傾向。

tension〔'tɛnʃən〕*n.*
緊張

There is always a feeling of *tension*
in the class before a big exam.
在大考之前，班上總會有一種緊張的感覺。

terminal〔'tɝmənḷ〕
n.（公車的）總站

The bus will depart at 6:15. Please
be at the *terminal* by 6:00.
公車會在六點十五分出發。請在六點之
前到達總站。

terminate〔'tɝmə͵net〕
v. 終止

When the two sides could not agree,
they decided to *terminate* the
discussion.
當雙方無法達成協議時，他們決定要終止
討論。

terrain〔tɛ'ren〕*n.*
地勢；地形

The ancient city was protected from
invasion by the mountainous *terrain*
that surrounded it.
環繞這座古老的城市的多山地形，保護了
這城市免於遭受侵略。

theater 〔'θiətɚ〕 *n.*
劇院；電影院

The play begins at 8:00, but it is a good idea to get to the *theater* a little earlier.
這場戲八點開演，但早點到達劇院是個好主意。

theory 〔'θiərɪ〕 *n.* 理論

The *theory* that the earth was flat was eventually proved false.
地球是平的這項理論，最後被證實是錯的。

thick 〔θɪk〕 *adj.* 厚的；充滿的

The sidewalks were *thick* with tourists waiting for the parade to begin. 人行道充滿了等待遊行開始的觀光客。

thorough 〔'θɝo〕 *adj.*
徹底的；完全的

The doctor gave the patient a *thorough* examination in order to discover the cause of his mysterious illness. 醫生替這位病人做了徹底的檢查，以便找出他神秘疾病的病因。

though 〔ðo〕 *conj.* 雖然
adv. 不過

The man refused our help *though* he was obviously lost. 這個人拒絕了我們的幫助，雖然他顯然是迷路了。

It will be sunny today; rain is predicted for tomorrow, *though*.
今天是晴朗的；不過根據預報，明天會下雨。

throughout (θru'aʊt)
prep. 遍及；在…各處

There is a lack of parking *throughout* the city.

這城市到處都缺乏停車位。

tin (tɪn) *adj.* 錫製的
n. 錫

These *tin* cans are recyclable.

這些錫罐是可以回收的。

tiny ('taɪnɪ) *adj.* 微小的

Give me only a *tiny* bit of that cake; I'm on a diet.

那個蛋糕只要給我很小一塊就好；我正在節食。

tip (tɪp) *n.* 尖端

He broke the *tip* of the pencil by pressing too hard when he was writing.

他在寫字時，因為壓得太用力，所以把鉛筆的筆尖折斷了。

tolerance ('tɑlərəns)
n. 容忍；忍受能力

The teacher does not have a lot of *tolerance* for noise, so he is always telling us to be quiet.

這位老師不太能忍受噪音，所以他總是告訴我們要安靜一點。

tolerant ('tɑlərənt)
adj. 寬容的

Grandparents are often more *tolerant* of a child's bad behavior than his parents are. 祖父母常比父母，更能容忍孩子不良的行為。

tolerate (ˈtɑləˌret) *v.*
容許;忍受

We were warned that the company did not *tolerate* lateness.
我們被警告說,這家公司不容許遲到。

She moved to a warmer climate because she could not *tolerate* the cold weather. 她搬到了較溫暖的地方,因爲她不能忍受寒冷的天氣。

torch (tɔrtʃ) *n.* (用於焊接的)氣炬;火把

The welder put on his goggles and lit the *torch*.
焊工戴上護目鏡,並點燃氣炬。

torpedo (tɔrˈpido)
n. 魚雷

The submarine fired a *torpedo* at the enemy ship.
潛水艇向敵艦發射魚雷。

tour (tur) *n.* 旅行
v. 巡視

We will take a *tour* of Europe during the summer vacation.
我們將在暑假期間到歐洲旅行。

The general will *tour* the base as part of his inspection.
將軍將會巡視基地,作爲其視察的一部份。

tourist (ˈturɪst) *n.*
觀光客;遊客

The *tourists* were tired after a long day of sightseeing.
在經過漫長的一日觀光後,遊客們都累了。

tower (ˈtauɚ) *n.*
塔;高樓

The old *tower* was once used by the king's soldiers to watch for enemy attacks.
這座古老的高塔,曾被國王的士兵用來監視敵軍的攻擊。

toxic (ˈtɑksɪk) *adj.*
有毒的

The man was poisoned by a *toxic* gas. 這個人因為吸入有毒的氣體而中毒。

trace (tres) *v.* 追溯;描繪

She *traced* the picture onto a thin piece of paper and then colored it herself. 她將美景描繪在一張薄紙上,然後自己塗上顏色。

The outbreak of food poisoning was *traced* back to a restaurant in the mall.
食物中毒事件的爆發,被追溯到購物中心的餐廳。

track (træk) *n.* 通道

You can follow this *track* back to the park entrance.
你可以順著這條通道,回到公園的入口。

trade (tred) *n.* 行業
v. 從事交易

People in the toy *trade* usually make large profits before Christmas and other holidays.
從事玩具業的人,在聖誕節和其他節日前,通常能賺取巨額的利潤。

train 〔 tren 〕 *v.* 訓練

The sergeant's primary responsibility is to *train* new troops.

那名中士的主要責任，就是訓練新的部隊。

training 〔'trenɪŋ 〕 *n.* 訓練

The new employees will be given *training* in how to handle company transactions.

新進員工將接受如何處理公司業務的訓練。

trait 〔 tret 〕 *n.* 特色

I am surprised he is late because punctuality is one of his *traits*.

我很驚訝他遲到了，因為守時是他的特色之一。

transfer 〔 træns'fɝ 〕 *v.* 轉移

When we got a new computer system we had to *transfer* all of our files to the new machines.

當我們有了新的電腦系統後，必須將所有的檔案轉移到新的機器裡。

```
trans  +  fer
  |         |
across  +  carry
```

transmitter 〔 træns'mɪtɚ 〕 *n.* 無線電發射機

We used the *transmitter* to send a message back to the base.

我們用無線電發射機，傳遞訊息回基地。

transport

〔 træns'port 〕 v. 運送；
運輸

The tour company will *transport* us
from the airport to our hotel.
旅遊公司會把我們從機場送到旅館。

transportation

〔 ,trænspə'teʃən 〕 n.
運輸工具

The MRT is the most popular form
of public *transportation* in the city.
捷運是這個城市中，最受歡迎的一種大眾
運輸工具。

trash 〔 træʃ 〕 n. 垃圾

The *trash* must be placed on the side
of the street before the garbage truck
arrives.
在垃圾車抵達之前，垃圾必須被放在街道
的旁邊。

tray 〔 tre 〕 n. 餐盤

After selecting his food, Bill carried
his *tray* to the cashier.
比爾挑完食物後，就拿著餐盤走向櫃台收
銀員。

tremendous

〔 trɪ'mɛndəs 〕 adj.
驚人的；巨大的

The noise of the explosion was
tremendous; it could be heard for
miles. 爆炸的聲音很驚人；幾英哩之外
都聽得見。

There was a *tremendous* turnout for
the presidential election.
總統大選的投票率很高。

trench 〔 trɛntʃ 〕 *n.* 戰壕

The soldiers dug a *trench* to protect themselves from enemy fire.
士兵們挖了一道戰壕，來保護自己免於敵人的砲火。

trigger 〔 'trɪgɚ 〕 *n.* 扳機

He pointed the gun at me and threatened to pull the *trigger*.
他用槍指著我，並威脅要扣下扳機。

trim 〔 trɪm 〕 *adj.* 苗條的

The doctor recommended that I get more exercise if I wanted to become *trim*. 醫生建議我，如果想變得苗條，就要多做一點運動。

troubleshoot
〔 'trʌbḷ,ʃut 〕 *v.* 解決困難；檢修

We called in an expert to *troubleshoot* the malfunctioning machine.
我們請了一位專家，來檢修故障的機器。

trust 〔 trʌst 〕 *v.* 信任

You can *trust* him to get the job done in time.
你可以信任他，會及時完成工作。

trustworthy
〔 'trʌst,wɝðɪ 〕 *adj.* 可靠的

I am not worried about lending you the money because I know that you are *trustworthy*.
我不擔心把錢借給你，因為我知道，你是很可靠的。

tubing (ˈtjubɪŋ) *n.*
橡皮管

These workers are responsible for installing the *tubing* in our appliances.
這些工人負責替我們的設備安裝橡皮管。

tunnel (ˈtʌnḷ) *n.* 隧道

To get across the river you may either take the bridge or drive through the *tunnel* that runs underneath it.
要橫越這條河，你要不是從橋上通過，就是開車從穿過河底的隧道通過。

turbine (ˈtɝbɪn) *n.*
渦輪機；渦輪

The accident was due to a problem with the new *turbine* engine.
這場意外事故，是由於新的渦輪引擎出問題。

turn (tɝn) *n.* 輪流的機會

It's your *turn* to take out the trash.
輪到你去倒垃圾了。

twist (twɪst) *v.* 扭曲

If you *twist* these two wires together, they will conduct electricity.
如果你將這兩條電線扭在一起，它們就能導電。

type (taɪp) *n.* 種類

This *type* of clothing is very flattering to you.
這類的衣服，很能突顯你的優點。

typewriter

(ˈtaɪpˌraɪtɚ) *n.* 打字機

We can type data more efficiently with a computer than with a *typewriter*.

我們用電腦打資料，比用打字機更有效率。

typical (ˈtɪpɪkḷ) *adj.*

典型的

He is a *typical* teenager and likes to play video games and basketball.

它是個典型的青少年，喜歡打電動玩具和打籃球。

【劉毅老師的話】

你對英文有瘋狂的興趣嗎？

歡迎你隨時來「劉毅英文」找我。

班址：台北市重慶南路一段 10 號 7F

U

uncomfortable

〔 ʌn'kʌmfɚtəbḷ 〕 *adj.*
不舒服的

The seats on those old buses are very *uncomfortable*.

那些舊巴士裡的座椅，坐起來很不舒服。

uncomfortably

〔 ʌn'kʌmfɚtəblɪ 〕 *adv.*
不舒服地

Because there were no free chairs, the boy sat *uncomfortably* on the edge of the table.

因為沒有空的椅子，所以這個男孩只好不舒服地坐在桌子的邊緣。

unconscious

〔 ʌn'kɑnʃəs 〕 *adj.*
無意識的；昏迷的

The driver of the car was *unconscious* when the rescuers found him.

當救援人員找到這部車的駕駛人時，他是昏迷的。

un	+	con	+	sci	+	ous
not	+	*with*	+	*know*	+	*adj.*

undergo 〔 ʌndɚ'go 〕
v. 接受

All the applicants were required to *undergo* a series of tests to determine whether or not they were suitable for the job.

所有的應徵者，都必須接受一系列的測試，以確定他們是否適合這份工作。

underneath

〔͵ʌndə'niθ 〕 *prep.*

在…之下

Rita hid the present *underneath* her bed.

麗塔將禮物藏在她的床下。

underwater

〔'ʌndə͵wɔtə 〕 *adv.*

在水面下

Because the submarine traveled *underwater*, the people onshore were unaware of its presence.

因為潛水艇是在水面下移動，所以岸上的人察覺不到它的存在。

unfriendly

〔 ʌn'frɛndlɪ 〕 *adj.*

不友善的

The salesclerk was very *unfriendly*, so I decided to go to another store.

這個店員非常不友善，所以我決定去另一家店。

unfurnished

〔 ʌn'fɝnɪʃt 〕 *adj.*

不附傢俱的

The rent is low because the apartment is *unfurnished*; we will have to spend more money on furniture.

這棟公寓因為不附傢俱所以房租便宜；我們得多花錢買傢俱。

uninsulated

〔 ʌn'ɪnsə͵letɪd 〕 *adj.*

未絕緣的

Touching an *uninsulated* wire is very dangerous.

碰到未絕緣的電線，是很危險的。

unit 〔'junɪt 〕 *n.* 單元

We finished *unit* three in class today.

今天在課堂上，我們上完了第三單元。

unite〔jʊ'naɪt〕*v.*
合併；使聯合

The boys' and girls' high school will *unite* next year; we will have one high school instead of two.

男校和女校將在明年合併；我們將會有一所高中，而不是兩所。

unless〔ən'lɛs〕*conj.*
除非

We will not make it to the train station in time *unless* we leave right now.

除非我們馬上離開，否則將無法及時趕到火車站。

unnecessary
〔ʌn'nɛsə͵sɛrɪ〕*adj.*
不必要的

Reservations are *unnecessary* during the week because the hotel is never full then.

平日不必預訂旅館，因為那時絕不會客滿。

unselfish〔ʌn'sɛlfɪʃ〕
adj. 不自私的

Our neighbor is an *unselfish* man who often gives his money and time to charity.

我們的鄰居是一個不自私的人，他常把時間和金錢投注在慈善事業上。

upper〔'ʌpɚ〕*adj.*
上方的

He chose to take the *upper* bunk when he moved into the new barracks.

當他搬進新的營房時，他選擇睡上舖。

urge 〔 ɝdʒ 〕 *v.* 力勸

Although I think I have little chance of succeeding, my teacher is ***urging*** me to apply to the best schools.
雖然我覺得我只有極小的成功機會，但我的老師還是力勸我申請最好的學校。

My doctor ***urged*** me to take better care of my health.
我的醫生勸我要更妥善地照顧自己的健康。

utilities 〔 ju'tɪlətɪz 〕
n. pl. 公用事業（ 如水、電、瓦斯等 ）

The ***utilities*** are included in the rent, so we do not have to worry about paying the gas and electric bills.
公用事業是包含在租金裡面，所以我們不必擔心要支付瓦斯和電費帳單。

utilize 〔 'jutḷ͵aɪz 〕 *v.* 利用

In order to pay for the repairs, the committee had to ***utilize*** the money set aside for the new gymnasium.
為了付修理費用，委員會必須動用為了興建新體育館所保留的款項。

V

vacuum (ˈvækjuəm)
n. 真空

Removing all the air from the chamber created a *vacuum*.
將所有的空氣自房間中除去，就創造出一個真空狀態。

vague (veg) *adj.* 模糊的

The bank teller was only able to give a *vague* description of the robber, so it is unlikely that the police will find him. 銀行出納員只能模糊地描述搶匪的相貌，所以警方不可能找到搶匪。

valley (ˈvælɪ) *n.* 山谷

The town is located in the *valley* between those two mountains.
這個城鎮是位於兩座山之間的山谷。

valuable (ˈvæljəbḷ)
adj. 珍貴的；有用的

The diamonds my grandmother gave me are very *valuable*.
我祖母給我的鑽石非常珍貴。

A part-time job can give a teenager some *valuable* experience.
打工可以給青少年有用的經驗。

value (ˈvælju) *n.* 價值；重要性

The *value* of good health cannot be overemphasized.
良好健康的重要性，再怎麼強調也不為過。

values (ˈvæljʊz) *n. pl.*
價值觀

People of different cultures
sometimes have different *values*.
不同文化背景的人，有時會有不同的價
值觀。

vanish (ˈvænɪʃ) *v.* 消失

To the controller's surprise, the plane
vanished from the radar screen.
令管制員驚訝的是，這架飛機從雷達螢幕
上消失了。

vapor (ˈvepɚ) *n.* 蒸氣

The water turned to *vapor* when it
was heated.
水受熱之後，就變成了水蒸氣。

vaporize (ˈvepəˌraɪz)
v. 蒸發

It was so hot that the rain *vaporized*
before it reached the ground.
天氣太熱，以致於雨還沒落到地面之前，
就蒸發了。

variable (ˈvɛrɪəbl̩)
adj. 會變動的

The weather today will be *variable*,
with both sunshine and rain.
今天天氣多變化，既會出太陽，也會下雨。

various (ˈvɛrɪəs) *adj.*
各種的

There are *various* resources in the
library, such as dictionaries,
encyclopedias, and a computer.
圖書館裡有各種資源，像是字典、百科全
書，和電腦。

vary〔'vɛrɪ〕*v.* 變化

The weather *varies* a lot in winter; sometimes it is warm and at other times it is quite cold.

冬天的天氣變化很大;有時溫暖,有時很冷。

vein〔ven〕*n.* 靜脈

The nurse took blood from a *vein* in the patient's arm.

護士從病人手臂上的靜脈抽血。

velocity〔və'lɑsətɪ〕*n.* 速度

The engineer was told to reduce the *velocity* of the train because there had been an accident on the track.

火車司機被告知須減緩車速,因為鐵軌上發生了意外事故。

verify〔'vɛrə,faɪ〕*v.* 證實;確認

The woman *verified* that it was indeed her husband's voice on the tape.

這名婦人證實,錄音帶裡的,的確是她丈夫的聲音。

```
ver  +  ify
 |       |
true  +  make
```

vessel〔'vɛsḷ〕*n.* 船

The *vessel* lost power while it was out at sea and had to radio for help.

那艘船出海時失去了動力,必須以無線電求救。

veteran (ˈvɛtərən)
n. 退役軍人

Because he is a *veteran*, he has the right to receive medical care at the army hospital.

因為他是一名退役軍人,所以有權利接受軍醫院的醫療照顧。

vibrate (ˈvaɪbret) *v.*
搖動

The plane began to *vibrate* due to the bad weather.

由於天候狀況不佳,所以飛機開始搖晃。

vice (vaɪs) *n.*
惡習;邪惡

Drinking too much is his greatest *vice*.

酒喝太多是他最大的惡習。

vicinity (vəˈsɪnətɪ)
n. 附近

It is important that we find a house with a good school in the *vicinity*.

在附近找到一間位於好學區的房子,對我們而言是很重要的。

victim (ˈvɪktɪm) *n.*
受害者

The police believe that the murder *victim* knew his killer.

警方相信,這起謀殺案的受害者知道誰是殺手。

view (vju) *n.* 景色

We climbed to the top of the mountain to look at the *view* from there.

我們爬上這座山的山頂,從那裡眺望景色。

viewpoint 〔'vju,pɔɪnt 〕
n. 觀點

I'm afraid I cannot understand your
viewpoint on this matter.
恐怕我無法了解你對這件事的觀點。

violin 〔,vaɪə'lɪn 〕 *n.*
小提琴

Stephen loves music and he has
played the *violin* since he was a child.
史蒂芬喜愛音樂，而且他從小就會拉小
提琴。

viscosity 〔 vɪs'kɑsətɪ 〕
n. 黏度

The *viscosity* of most oils will
increase as they become colder, and
then they will pour more slowly.
大多數的油在冷卻時黏度會增加，然後流
出的速度會更慢。

vision 〔'vɪʒən 〕 *n.* 視力

My brother needs to wear glasses to
correct his *vision*.
我弟弟需要戴眼鏡來矯正他的視力。

visual 〔'vɪʒuəl 〕 *adj.*
視覺的

The salesman used a lot of *visual*
aids in his presentation. 這名推銷員
在介紹時，使用了許多視覺輔助工具。

vital 〔'vaɪtḷ 〕 *adj.*
非常重要的

This medicine is a *vital* part of the
WHO plan to help people in
developing countries.
在世界衛生組織要協助開發中國家的計
劃中，這種藥是極為重要的一部份。

voice 〔 vɔɪs 〕 *n.* 聲音

He has a loud *voice* and can easily be heard in any gathering.

他的聲音宏亮，在任何集會中，都能輕易地聽見。

volt 〔 volt 〕 *n.* 伏特

Power lines can carry thousands of *volts* of electricity.

電線可以傳送好幾千伏特的電流。

voltage 〔'voltɪdʒ 〕 *n.* 電壓

The electrical toy is considered safe because it emits only a low *voltage*.

這種電動的玩具被認為是安全的，因為它只會發出低電壓。

volume 〔'vɑljəm 〕 *n.* 音量

Please turn up the *volume* on the TV; I can hardly hear it.

請將電視的音量開大聲；我幾乎聽不到。

vote 〔 vot 〕 *v.* 投票

A large number of people turned out to *vote* in the last election.

在上一次的選舉時，有許多人出去投票。

W

warfare ('wɔr,fɛr) *n.*
戰爭

The dispute over the border will lead to *warfare* if it is not resolved soon.
關於邊界的爭議若沒有馬上解決，可能會導致戰爭。

warrant ('wɔrənt)
n. 授權；批准

He holds the rank of *warrant* officer in the navy.
他擁有海軍士官長的官階。

warship ('wɔr,ʃɪp)
n. 軍艦

The *warship* was involved in training exercises in the Pacific Ocean.
這艘軍艦有參與太平洋的訓練演習。

waste (west) *n.* 廢棄物
v. 浪費

The factory is being investigated because it dumps its *waste* directly into the river. 這家工廠因為直接將廢棄物傾倒在河裡，而正在接受調查。

It is important not to *waste* water during a drought.
在乾旱時期，不浪費水是非常重要的。

waterproof
('wɔtɚ'pruf) *adj.* 防水的

You can use this camera to take pictures in the water because it is *waterproof*. 你可以在水裡用這台相機拍照，因為它是防水的。

watertight
(ˈwɔtɚˈtaɪt) *adj.* 防水的

It's a good idea to store your valuables in a *watertight* container when you travel by boat. 當你乘船旅行時,把貴重物品存放在防水容器內,是個好主意。

wave (wev) *n.*
波浪;波

The little boy cried when he was knocked down by a large *wave* at the beach. 當這個小男孩在沙灘上被大浪推倒時,他哭了起來。

Sonar uses sound *waves* to detect objects. 聲納是利用音波來偵測物體。

wavy (ˈwevɪ) *adj.*
波浪形的

Isabel has long, *wavy* hair.
伊莎貝爾有一頭波浪形的長髮。

wealth (wɛlθ) *n.*
財富;財產

He is a man of great *wealth*, but he has little time to enjoy his money.
他是個擁有龐大財產的人,但他沒有多少時間享受他的金錢。

weight (wet) *n.* 啞鈴

Tim uses *weights* when he exercises.
提姆運動時會使用啞鈴。

weld (wɛld) *v.* 焊接

We must *weld* the two pieces of metal together to repair the machine.
要修好這台機器,我們必須把這兩塊金屬焊接在一起。

wheat ﹝hwit﹞ *n.* 小麥

Most of the farmers in this region grow *wheat*.

在這個地區，大多數的農民都種植小麥。

when ﹝hwɛn﹞ *adv.* 當…時候

He got very good grades *when* he was in high school.

他唸高中的時候，成績很好。

where ﹝hwɛr﹞ *conj.* …的地方

Alan lives in a neighborhood *where* there are a lot of trees.

艾倫住的地方，附近有很多樹。

wild ﹝waɪld﹞ *adj.* 野生的；瘋狂的

It is not safe to approach *wild* animals such as bears and tigers.

靠近像熊和老虎這樣的野生動物，是很不安全的。

He went *wild* with grief after the death of his son. 在他兒子死後，他悲痛欲絕。

wilderness ﹝'wɪldənɪs﹞ *n.* 荒野

The hikers camped in the *wilderness* during their trip. 在這次的旅途中，這些徒步旅行者，在荒野中露營。

willing ﹝'wɪlɪŋ﹞ *adj.* 願意的

He was not *willing* to work the night shift and asked for the first shift instead.

他不願意上晚班，而要求換成第一班。

wind〔waɪnd〕*v.* 捲繞；
蜿蜒而流；上緊發條

It takes a lot of skill to sail on the river because it *winds* across the plain instead of going in a straight line.
要在這條河上航行需要高超的技巧，因為這條河不是直的，而是沿著平原蜿蜒而流。

My watch stopped because I forgot to *wind* it. 我的手錶停了，因為我忘記把它的發條上緊。

windscreen
〔'wɪnd,skrin〕*n.*
擋風玻璃

The pilot had a clear view of the runway through the *windscreen*.
這名飛行員透過擋風玻璃，可以很清楚地看到跑道。

windshield
〔'wɪnd,ʃild〕*n.* 擋風玻璃

Because the driver wasn't wearing a seat belt, he hit the *windshield* when he ran into the fence.
由於這名駕駛人沒有繫上安全帶，所以當他撞到圍牆時，頭撞上了擋風玻璃。

wing〔wɪŋ〕*n.* 機翼；
翅膀

Ice had to be removed from the *wings* of the plane before it could take off.
必須先將機翼的冰塊除去，飛機才能起飛。

The bird injured its *wing* and was no longer able to fly. 這隻鳥傷了自己的翅膀，所以再也飛不起來了。

wire 〔 waɪr 〕 *n.* 電線

A broken *wire* was the cause of the electrical failure.
電線損壞是導致停電的原因。

wiring 〔 'waɪrɪŋ 〕 *n.* 配線

We called in an electrician to repair the faulty *wiring* in the house.
我們請了一位電工，來修理這棟房子內不完善的配線。

within 〔 wɪð'ɪn 〕 *prep.* 在…之內

The train will arrive *within* ten minutes. 火車會在十分鐘之內到達。

He prefers to live *within* the city limits.
他比較喜歡住在市區內。

withstand 〔 wɪθ'stænd 〕 *v.* 抵抗；經得起

After the earthquake, the residents were told to evacuate because their house would not be able to *withstand* another shock. 地震過後，居民們被要求疏散，因為他們的房子經不起再一次的震動。

wonder 〔 'wʌndɚ 〕 *v.* 想知道

I *wonder* what time the movie starts. I'll call the theater and ask. 我想知道電影何時開演。我會打電話去電影院查詢。

workshop 〔 'wɝkˌʃɑp 〕 *n.* 小工廠

The carpenter has his own *workshop*, which is where he does most of his work. 這名木匠有自己的小工廠，他大部分的工作都在那裡完成。

worse 〔wɜs〕*adj.*
更糟的

You may not be good at playing the piano, but I am even *worse*.
你可能不擅長彈鋼琴，可是我彈得更糟。

worst 〔wɜst〕*adj.*
最差的

Peter is the *worst* tennis player on the team. 彼得是隊上最差勁的網球選手。

worth 〔wɜθ〕*adj.*
值得的　*n.* 價值

The jewelry is kept in the safe because it is *worth* a lot of money.
這些珠寶被放在保險箱裡，因為值很多錢。

wound 〔wund〕*n.*
傷口　*v.* 使受傷

Although the *wound* looked serious, the doctor said it would not require stitches. 雖然這個傷口看起來很嚴重，但醫生說不需要縫合。

The trainee was *wounded* during target practice.
這名新兵是在射擊練習時受傷的。

wrap 〔ræp〕*v.*
包；裹

We still have to *wrap* the presents before the party.
我們還是必須在宴會前，將禮物包裝好。

wreck 〔rɛk〕*v.*
毀壞；使失敗

The earthquake *wrecked* many buildings in the downtown area.
這次的地震，破壞了許多位於市中心地區的建築物。

X/Z

X-ray 〔'ɛksˌre 〕 *n.*
X 光片　*v.* 以 X 光檢查

The doctor took an ***X-ray*** to see whether or not my arm was broken.
醫生照了 X 光片，來確認我的手臂是否有骨折。

We will need to ***X-ray*** you to see whether your ribs are broken or merely bruised.
我們需要幫你照 X 光，來檢查你的肋骨是否有骨折，還是只有瘀傷。

yet 〔 jɛt 〕 *conj.* 但是

The performance was not very good, ***yet*** the audience clapped anyway.
這場演出不太出色，但是無論如何，觀眾還是鼓掌了。

zone 〔 zon 〕 *n.* 區域

You cannot build a factory in a residential ***zone***.
你不能在住宅區建工廠。

ECL 片語總整理

a green thumb
園藝的才能

Tina really has *a green thumb*; her garden always looks beautiful.
蒂娜確實有園藝的才能；她的花園看起來總是很美。

above all 最重要的是

It is important to drive carefully and, *above all*, follow the traffic rules.
小心開車是很重要的，而且最重要的是，要遵守交通規則。

account for 說明

The clerk could not *account for* the difference between his calculations and those of the customer.
這名店員無法說明，他和顧客的計算，為何有差異。

adhere to 黏著；遵守

The poster fell off the wall because the type of glue you used will not *adhere to* wood.
海報從牆上掉下來，因為你用的那種膠水沒辦法黏在木頭上。

Although he agreed to the rules of the game, he did not *adhere to* them.
雖然他贊成這些比賽規則，但卻沒有遵守。

adjust to 適應

It is often difficult for students to *adjust to* a new school.
學生們通常很難適應新的學校。

air conditioner
冷氣機

We often use the *air conditioner* during the summer months.
在夏天的那幾個月，我們常使用冷氣機。

air conditioning
空調設備

We decided not to rent that apartment because it does not have *air conditioning*.
我們決定不租那間公寓，因為它沒有空調設備。

airman basic
（美國）空軍列兵

The uniform of an *airman basic* carries no insignia.
空軍列兵的制服上，沒有佩帶勳章。

airman first class
（美國）空軍一等兵

Henry was recently promoted from the rank of airman to that of *airman first class*.
亨利最近從空軍列兵，晉升為空軍一等兵。

all at once 突然地

I was running through the park when *all at once* I felt a sharp pain in my leg. 當我跑過公園時，我的腿突然感到劇烈的疼痛。

all by *oneself* 獨自

John refused our help and finished the job *all by himself*.

約翰拒絕了我們的幫忙，獨自完成了這個工作。

all in all 大致上

Unfortunately, it rained during our vacation at the beach, but *all in all*, we had a good time.

遺憾的是，我們在海灘渡假時，一直下雨，但大致上，我們還是玩得很愉快。

along with 連同

Chemistry, *along with* mathematics, is a difficult subject for me.

化學和數學對我而言，都是困難的科目。

alongside of
在⋯旁邊

The child stood *alongside of* his mother. 這個小孩站在他母親身邊。

approve of
同意；批准

The manager did not *approve of* the salesman's habit of making personal phone calls at the office.

經理對這名業務員，在辦公室裡打私人電話的習慣，感到不滿。

The committee is still considering our proposal, but I am certain that they will *approve of* it.

委員會還在考慮我們的提案，但是我確定，他們會批准這個提案。

armed forces
（陸、海、空）三軍部隊

The *armed forces* include both the army and navy.
三軍部隊包含陸軍和海軍。

as a result 因此

Jim failed the final exam; *as a result*, he will have to repeat the course.
吉姆期末考不及格；因此他必須重修這門課。

as a result of 由於

Many buildings were damaged *as a result of* the earthquake.
由於地震的關係，有許多建築物受損。

as though 好像

She just broke up with her boyfriend, but she acts *as though* she doesn't care. 她剛跟男朋友分手，但卻表現得像是不在乎的樣子。

as well as 以及；
和～一樣好

He can play the piano *as well as* the guitar.
他彈鋼琴的技巧，和彈吉他一樣好。

assume responsibility
承擔責任

We had to *assume responsibility* for the goods when we signed for them.
當我們簽收這些商品後，就必須為其承擔責任。

at a time 一次

It's not a difficult job if we do it one step *at a time*.
如果我們一步一步地做，這個工作並不難。

The sergeant told the men to come in two *at a time*.
中士告訴士兵們，一次進來兩個。

at least 至少

We need *at least* three people to play this card game.
我們至少需要三個人，才能玩牌。

Even if we fail, we will gain some valuable experience *at least*.
即使是失敗，我們至少會獲得一些寶貴的經驗。

at once 立刻

The ticket agent told me to go to the gate *at once* because the flight was about to leave.
機票代售業者要我立刻前往登機門，因為飛機即將起飛了。

back and forth
來回地

The man walked *back and forth* along the sidewalk, looking for the money he had dropped.
這名男子沿著人行道走來走去，尋找剛才掉落的錢。

bare wire 裸露的電線

Be sure to turn off the electricity before you touch that *bare wire*.
在你碰觸裸露的電線之前，一定要確定，已經把電源關掉了。

basic training （新兵的）基本訓練

Soldiers practice on the firing range as part of their *basic training*.
在靶場練習，是新兵基本訓練的一部份。

be about to 正要

They *were about to* close the store when a customer walked in.
當一位顧客走進來時，他們正打算要關店。

be assigned to 被分派到

The recruit hopes to *be assigned to* an overseas post after he completes his training. 這名新兵希望在完成訓練課程後，能被分派到海外的駐紮地。

be behind in 遲的；逾期未付的

The landlord threatened to evict Robert because he *is behind in* the rent. 房東威脅要將羅伯特趕出去，因為他的房租逾期未繳。

be born 出生

Dave *was born* in the country, but his family moved to the city when he was quite young.
戴夫在鄉下出生，但在他很小的時候，全家就搬到城市裡了。

be charged with
被指控

The man *is charged with* murder and he will be held in jail until his trial.

這名男子被控謀殺，所以直到被審判之前，他都會被關在拘留所。

be composed of
由…組成

Water *is composed of* hydrogen and oxygen.

水是由氫和氧所組成。

be fed up with
對～感到厭煩

The boss *is fed up with* Dan's lateness and has threatened to fire him.

老闆對丹的遲到感到厭煩，威脅要開除他。

be in contact with
和～聯繫

The pilot *was in contact with* the control tower.

這名飛行員和塔台有聯繫。

be in on 參與

Adam wants to *be in on* the preparations for the party.

亞當想要參與宴會的準備工作。

be in touch with
和…取得聯繫

I have lost track of my high school friend; I am not *in touch with* him anymore.

我和我高中時的朋友已經失去聯絡了；我再也沒有跟他取得聯繫。

be no use 沒有用的

It *is no use* trying to change his mind because he is very stubborn.

試著要他改變想法是沒有用的，因爲他很固執。

be promoted 晉升

The lieutenant hopes to *be promoted* when he is reassigned.

這名中尉希望在被重新指派工作時，能獲得晉升。

be stationed 被派駐

The sergeant *was stationed* at the front during the war.

這名中士在戰爭時，被派駐在前線。

be to 必須…；預定…

All new recruits *are to* report to the base no later than 0800 hours.

所有的新兵，必須在八點之前向基地報到。

The ceremony *is to* be held outdoors.

這場典禮預定在戶外舉行。

be unable to 無法

I am sorry, but I *am unable to* attend your party because I have a previous commitment.

很抱歉，我無法參加你的宴會，因爲我有約在先。

be up for 被考慮

The corporal will *be up for* a promotion after he completes this tour of duty.

這名下士在服完這期兵役後，會被列入考慮，是否會晉升。

be up on 熟悉

Why don't you ask Frank what to do? He's *up on* the new regulations.

你何不問問法蘭克該麼辦？他熟知新的規定。

be up to 能做；是…的義務；由…決定

Pamela is not *up to* playing tennis today because she has a cold.

潘蜜拉今天不能打網球，因爲她感冒了。

Whether or not we have to work tomorrow is *up to* the manager.

我們明天是否要上班，是由經理決定的。

because of 因爲

The harvest is poor this year *because of* the lack of rain.

今年歉收，是因爲雨量不足。

bed rest 臥床休息

The doctor ordered *bed rest* for the patient until his fever broke.

醫生指示這名病人要臥床休息，直到退燒爲止。

believe in 相信…的
價值

The athlete ***believes in*** getting at least one hour of exercise every day.
這名運動員相信，每天至少做一小時的運動是有益的。

be subject to 須服從…的；易於…的

All citizens ***are subject to*** the laws of the country.
所有的國民都必須服從國家的法律。

Prices ***are subject to*** change without notice. 價格常會無預警地變動。

blood pressure 血壓

The doctor took my ***blood pressure*** as part of the physical exam.
醫生替我量血壓，那是身體檢查的一部份。

blow out 吹熄

Don't ***blow out*** the candles until you have made a wish.
在你許願之前，別將蠟燭吹熄。

blow up 炸毀

The terrorist threatened to ***blow up*** the bus.
恐怖份子威脅說，要炸毀這輛巴士。

We will ***blow up*** the abandoned building as part of our training.
炸毀這棟廢棄建築物，是我們訓練的一部份。

break down 故障；
分解

The room became very hot when the air conditioner ***broke down***.
當冷氣機故障時，這個房間變得很熱。

The chemist was able to ***break down*** the drug and analyze its components.
這名藥劑師能將藥物分解，並分析它的成份。

break in (on) 打斷；
插嘴

They were talking so excitedly that it was difficult to ***break in*** and explain what happened.
他們談得太興奮了，以致於很難插嘴解釋發生了什麼事。

brigadier general
（美國陸軍、空軍或海軍陸戰隊）准將

Everyone on the base is nervous about the ***brigadier general***'s upcoming inspection. 這個基地的每一個人，對於准將要來視察，都感到很緊張。

bring about 導致；
造成

The flood was ***brought about*** by a series of thunderstorms.
這次的水災，是由一連串的雷雨所造成的。

bring up 提出（問題）；撫養長大

The couple decided to ***bring up*** their children in the country.
這對夫婦決定要在鄉下，把他們的孩子撫養長大。

by accident 偶然地；意外地	I picked up his pen *by accident*; I certainly didn't intend to take it. 我是偶然撿起他的筆；我當然沒打算拿走它。
by chance 偶然地	We found this restaurant *by chance* while we were taking a drive. 當我們駕車出遊時，偶然發現了這家餐廳。
by hand 用手	It is more personal to write a letter *by hand* than to type it. 用手寫信，比用打字機打更直接。
by means of 藉由	We are able to send e-mail messages *by means of* the computer. 我們能夠利用電腦，傳送電子郵件的訊息。
by the time 到了…的時候	The building had already burned down *by the time* the fire truck arrived. 當消防車抵達的時候，這棟建築物早已被燒毀。
by way of 經由	The tour group went to Europe *by way of* New York. 這個旅行團經由紐約到達歐洲。
call down 嚴厲責備	I had to *call* him *down* for taking my car without permission. 他沒有經過我的允許就開走我的車，我得嚴厲責備他。

call in 請⋯來

We will have to *call in* a plumber because we cannot repair the pipe ourselves.

我們必須請水管工人來，因為我們不會自己修水管。

call off 取消

If the other team does not arrive soon, we will have to *call off* the game.

如果另一隊無法馬上到達，我們就必須取消比賽。

call on 拜訪

We decided to *call on* Mrs. Williams because we hadn't seen her for over a month.

我們決定去拜訪威廉斯夫人，因為我們已經一個多月沒見過她了。

calm down 平靜下來

The police asked the witness to *calm down* and tell them what happened.

警方要求目擊者平靜下來，並告訴他們發生了什麼事。

carbon dioxide 二氧化碳

Although we exhale *carbon dioxide*, if we breathe too much of it in, it can harm us.

雖然我們呼出的是二氧化碳，但如果我們吸入過量的二氧化碳，可能會對我們造成傷害。

carry on 繼續

We decided to *carry on* with the hike despite the rain.
儘管下雨，我們還是決定要繼續健行。

carry out 完成

I was not able to *carry out* the task of typing the report because I ran out of paper.
我無法完成打這篇報告的工作，因為我的紙用完了。

catch on 明白；理解

I had to review the lesson three times before I *caught on*.
我必須複習這個課程三次，才能理解。

catch up with 追上；趕上

I ran as fast as I could, but I could not *catch up with* Tim and he won the race.
我儘可能跑快一點，但還是追不上提姆，所以他贏了比賽。

He missed a week of school and he is finding it difficult to *catch up with* the class. 他缺了一星期的課，所以他覺得要趕上班上同學很難。

catch up (on) 趕上
（落後的工作等）

I have a lot of work to *catch up on* after my vacation. 我在假期過後，有許多落後的工作進度要趕。

chain of command
指揮系統；行政管理系統

The soldiers hope to move up in the *chain of command* by getting a promotion. 這些士兵希望能獲得升遷，晉升到指揮系統裡。

check off 打上√記號；打上核對無誤記號

The teacher *checked off* the names of the students as he called the roll. 老師點名時，會在點過的學生名字上做記號。

check out 查看

After hearing about the new restaurant, I decided to *check* it *out*. 在聽到有關這家新餐廳的消息後，我決定去看一看。

check out on 符合要求；通過

It is the job of a driving instructor to *check* his students *out on* the controls of the car. 汽車教練的工作，就是要讓他的學生，能符合操控汽車的要求。

check up on 調查；檢查；核對

The clerk decided to *check up on* the missing shipment. 這名職員決定要調查，那批下落不明的貨物的去向。

If Paul said he will do the work, he will; it is not necessary to *check up on* him. 如果保羅說他會做這項工作，他就一定會；不必去調查他。

cheer up 使高興

Let's go visit Tom in the hospital and *cheer* him *up*.
我們去醫院探望湯姆，讓他高興一點。

chief master sergeant
（美國空軍）一級士官長
（士官最高階級）

Chief master sergeant is a rank in the air force.
一級士官長是空軍的一個階級。

chief petty officer
海軍士官長

My brother is a *chief petty officer* in the navy.
我哥哥是海軍士官長。

chief warrant officer
（美國陸海空軍及海岸
警衛隊的）一級准尉

The rank of *chief warrant officer* exists in the navy, marines and army.
一級准尉這個階級，海軍、海軍陸戰隊，和陸軍都有。

chip in 共同出錢；
捐助；湊錢

If everyone *chips in* one dollar, we can buy a subscription to the magazine for the class.
如果每個人出一元，我們就可以替班上訂這本雜誌。

chop down 砍倒

The tree was dead, so we decided to *chop* it *down*.
這棵樹已經枯死了，所以我們決定將它砍下來。

Class A uniform
A 級制服；大禮服；
最正式的服裝

The men were told to wear *Class A uniforms* for the parade.
士兵們被告知，遊行時必須穿著 A 級制服。

clear away 收拾；清除

After the snowstorm we had to *clear away* the snow from the driveway.
暴風雪過後，我們必須清除車道上的雪。

come across 偶然發現；偶然遇見

I *came across* this story in a magazine.
我在雜誌上偶然發現這個故事。

come along 一起去

Ask Joan if she wants to *come along* to the movies.
問瓊恩是否要一起去看電影。

come by 順道拜訪

Please *come by* and see us tomorrow.
明天請順道過來看看我們。

come down with 罹患

If you don't take better care of yourself, you may *come down with* a cold.
如果你不更加好好照顧自己，你可能會罹患感冒。

come out （花）開；（樹木）長新葉

The leaves on this tree usually *come out* in February.
這棵樹的葉子，通常會在二月份長出來。

come over　過來

If you *come over* around six o'clock, we can have dinner together.

如果你在六點鐘左右過來，我們就可以一起吃晚餐。

come to　共計

The dress and the jacket *come to* $75. Will that be cash or charge?

這件洋裝和那件夾克共計七十五元。要付現還是刷卡？

come up with　想出

How did you *come up with* such a great idea?

你是如何想出這麼棒的點子？

commissioned officer　軍官（ = *officer* ）

A *commissioned officer* holds higher rank than an NCO.

軍官的階級比士官還高。

count on　依賴

You can *count on* me to keep the secret; I won't tell a soul.

你可以依賴我幫你保守秘密；我不會告訴別人。

course of action　行動方針

After discussing the problem, we came up with a *course of action*.

在討論過這個問題之後，我們想出了一個行動方針。

cross ~ off… 將~
自…劃掉

After washing the car, he *crossed* that *off* his list of things to do. 在洗完車後，他從待處理事項表中，將這項工作劃掉。

cross out 劃掉

Please don't just *cross out* your mistakes on the test; erase them instead. 請不要只是劃掉你考卷上的錯誤；請把它們擦掉。

cut down (on) 減少

Judy plans to *cut down on* sweets in order to lose weight. 為了減重，茱蒂計劃要少吃甜食。

cut in 打斷（別人的話）；插嘴

I'm sorry to *cut in*, but you have an important phone call. 很抱歉打斷你們談話，但你有一通重要的來電。

cut off 切斷

The electricity was *cut off* during the storm. 在暴風雨期間，電力被切斷了。

dead wire 無法通電的電線

The machine did not work because there was a *dead wire* in the electrical system. 機器無法運轉，因為電力系統中，有電線無法通電。

deal with 討論;處理	The report ***deals with*** the problem of recycling. 這個報告是討論資源回收的問題。 I'm not sure how to ***deal with*** this problem. Can you help me? 我不確定該如何處理這個問題。你能幫我嗎?
depend on 依賴	I can't ***depend on*** my car; it's always breaking down. 我無法信賴我的車;它老是拋錨。
despite the fact that 雖然	***Despite the fact that*** John turned in his paper a day late, the professor gave him an A. 雖然約翰的報告遲交一天,教授還是給他 A。
die down 逐漸熄滅;變弱	We should let the campfire ***die down*** before we go to sleep. 在我們睡覺之前,應該讓營火逐漸熄滅。 The weather forecaster says that the typhoon will ***die down*** and become a tropical storm before morning. 氣象預報員說,颱風將會減弱,並且在早上之前,轉爲熱帶風暴。

dispose of 處理；除去

You should *dispose of* the battery in a special place.
你應該將電池丟在一個特殊的地方。

drill instructor
教官

The *drill instructor* will ask you to do things over and over again.
教官會再三地要求你做事情。

drop by 順道拜訪

John said he might *drop by* this afternoon to see our new car.
約翰說，他今天下午可能會順道來拜訪我們，看看我們的新車。

drop in 順道拜訪

As long as we are in the neighborhood, why don't we *drop in* and see Sarah?
既然我們就在附近，何不順道去拜訪莎拉？

drop off 把…放下；
睡著

Please *drop* these books *off* at the library on your way home.
麻煩在你回家途中，將這些書放在圖書館裡。

drop out of 退出

The candidate decided to *drop out of* the race for mayor when it became obvious that he would not win.
當這名候選人顯然無法贏得市長大選時，他決定退出這場競選。

drop over 順道拜訪

Beverly will *drop over* and see us tomorrow if she has time.
如果貝芙麗有空，她明天會順道來拜訪我們。

due to 由於

There is no school today *due to* the typhoon.
由於颱風來襲，所以今天不用上學。

during the time (that) 在…時候

During the time of peace, the villagers lived a happy life.
在太平時期，村民們過著快樂的生活。

My father was working abroad *during the time* that I attended junior high school.
當我就讀國中時，我爸爸正在國外工作。

each other 彼此；互相

We always give *each other* presents at Christmas.
我們總是在聖誕節時，互相送禮物。

end up 最後（成為）

He is such a good leader that he might *end up* president of the country one day.
他是一位非常傑出的領導者，也許有一天，他最後會成為這個國家的總統。

even if 即使

That test was so difficult that I wouldn't have passed it *even if* I had studied all night.

這個考試太難了,即使我整夜唸書,也無法及格。

even so 即使如此

It is impossible to finish this work by Monday. *Even so*, we must try to do it.

要在星期一完成這個工作,是不可能的。但即使如此,我們還是必須盡力去做。

Tom is not very good at baseball, but he was chosen for the team *even so*.

湯姆並不是很擅長打棒球,但即使如此,他還是被挑選加入球隊。

even though 即使;
雖然

Wendy thanked her aunt for the gift *even though* she didn't like it.

雖然溫蒂不喜歡這個禮物,她仍然為此向她阿姨致謝。

fall apart 散開;瓦解

This book is so old that it is about to *fall apart*.

這本書舊到快散開了。

fall in 集合;排隊

The sergeant ordered the men to *fall in* and march back to the base.

中士命令士兵們排隊,並行軍回到基地。

fight off 擊退；克服；
竭力擺脫

The army *fought off* the enemy forces
and saved the town.
這支軍隊擊退了敵軍，拯救了這個城鎮。

Tom is *fighting off* a cold because
he can't afford to get sick now.
湯姆正在治療感冒，因爲他現在不能生病。

Henry *fought off* the temptation to eat
the chocolate cake because he was on
a diet. 亨利克服了想吃巧克力蛋糕的
慾望，因爲他正在節食。

figure out 想出；理解

Can you help me? I can't *figure out*
how to work this machine.
你可以幫幫我嗎？我不知道該如何操作
這部機器。

find *one's* **way**
找出道路

I used a compass to *find my way*
through the mountains.
我利用指南針，來找到穿越山區的路。

firing pin
（槍砲的）撞針

The weapon did not fire because the
firing pin was defective.
這件武器無法發射，因爲它的撞針有問題。

firing range 靶場

The recruits went to the *firing range*
for target practice.
這些新兵到靶場去練習打靶。

first aid　急救

The paramedics gave the unconscious man *first aid*.

護理人員為這個昏迷的人急救。

first of all　首先

First of all, we need to find out how to get there, and then we can figure out what time we should leave.

首先,我們必須知道如何到那裡,然後再算出,該什麼時候出發。

first sergeant　士官長

The rank of *first sergeant* exists in both the army and the marine corps.

士官長這個階級,在陸軍和海軍陸戰隊都有。

fix up　裝修;整理

The house will be beautiful after we *fix* it *up*.

這棟房子在我們裝修過後,會變得很美。

for a living　謀生

What does your father do *for a living*?

你的父親是靠什麼謀生?

for example　例如

George is not very responsible. *For example*, he often forgets appointments.

喬治不是個非常負責的人。例如,他常忘記跟別人的約會。

from now on 從現
在開始

The semester is over. *From now on*
I can relax. 這學期結束了。從現在開
始，我可以輕鬆一下了。

garbage disposal
（裝在洗碗槽底的）垃圾
處理機

There are a lot of modern appliances
in the apartment, including a *garbage
disposal*. 這棟公寓有許多現代化的家
電用品，其中包括垃圾處理機。

**get a prescription
filled** 按處方籤配藥

The doctor said I can *get this
prescription filled* at the pharmacy
on the corner. 醫生說，我可以拿這張
處方籤，到轉角處的藥局配藥。

get across 使…被了解

The teacher tried to *get across* the
basic concepts of physics. 老師試著
使我們了解，這些物理學的基本概念。

get ahead 超前；成功

If you really want to *get ahead* in
this field, you should receive as
much training as possible.
如果你真的想在這個領域中超前，就應該
儘可能多接受訓練。

get behind in
在…落後

If you *get behind in* your work, it will
be very difficult for you to catch up.
如果你的工作進度落後，要趕上進度將會
很困難。

get by 以…勉強度過；
勉強及格

The clerk finds it difficult to *get by* on such a low income.

這名店員覺得，要靠這麼低的收入過日子，很困難。

Tim does not work hard in class; he does just enough to *get by*.

提姆在班上並不用功；他只做到足以勉強及格的地步。

get down 下降；降低

The winter was very warm; the temperature never even *got down* to 10 degrees. 這個冬天非常溫暖；氣溫甚至沒有降到十度以下過。

The doctor told Jim that he had to *get* his weight *down* or he would face serious health problems in the future.

醫生告訴吉姆，他必須減重，否則將來會面臨嚴重的健康問題。

get in 到達

What time will the first train *get in* tomorrow morning?

明天早上的第一班火車，何時會抵達？

get in contact with 和…聯絡

I lost Mary's phone number and now I don't know how to *get in contact with* her. 我弄丟了瑪麗的電話號碼，所以我現在不知道如何和她聯絡。

get in touch with
與…取得聯繫

I will *get in touch with* my relatives as soon as I arrive.

我一到達，就會與我的親戚取得聯繫。

get on with 繼續

After a short break, we will *get on with* our work.

在短暫的休息之後，我們將繼續做我們的工作。

get *one's* hands on
把…弄到手

All the telephones are in use now, but as soon as I can *get my hands on* one, I'll call the office.

所有的電話現在都在使用中，但只要我一搶到電話，我就會打電話到公司去。

get over 自（疾病中）
復原

It took me almost a month to *get over* my cold.

我花了將近一個月的時間，才從感冒中復原。

get through (with, to) 完成；以電話聯絡上

We cannot possibly *get through with* all this work today.

我們不可能在今天完成所有的工作。

I conldn't *get through to* my family because the phone is out of order.

我沒辦法用電話聯絡上我的家人，因為電話故障了。

give *sb.* **a hand**
幫忙某人

I can *give* you *a hand* with that suitcase.
我可以幫你提那個手提箱。

give in (to)
（向…）屈服

Iris was on a diet but she *gave in to* temptation and had a piece of cake.
愛麗絲正在節食，但她卻向誘惑屈服，而吃了一塊蛋糕。

give out 分發；散發

John, please *give out* the test papers to the class.
約翰，請將考卷發給全班同學。

This lamp does not *give out* a bright enough light.
這盞燈無法散發出夠亮的光線。

give up 放棄；停止

John decided to *give up* because it was obvious that he was going to lose the game. 約翰決定放棄，因為他顯然會輸掉這場比賽。

The doctor said I must *give up* playing tennis until my arm is completely healed. 醫生說，我必須停止打網球，直到我的手臂完全痊癒為止。

go ahead 繼續進行

We will *go ahead* with the celebration whether the guest of honor arrives **or** not. 無論貴賓是否到達，我們都將繼續進行這個慶祝活動。

go by 經過；依照

I need to *go by* the post office and mail this letter.
我必須經過郵局，寄這封信。

If you *go by* the advice in the guidebook, you won't get lost.
如果你依照旅遊指南上的建議，你就不會迷路了。

go on (with)
繼續（工作等）

John *went on* working after all of his colleagues had gone home.
約翰在所有的同事都回家後，還繼續工作。

The captain told the men to *go on with* their work even though it was time for dinner.
即使晚餐時間已經到了，船長還是告訴船員們，要繼續工作。

go out
熄滅；停止運轉

The electricity *went out* last night during the thunderstorm.
昨晚下雷雨時，停止供電。

go over 檢查;走過去

Remember to *go over* your answers before handing in the test paper.
在你交考卷之前,記得檢查你的答案。

I plan to *go over* to the library after class. 我打算下課後到圖書館去。

go right 進展順利

If everything *goes right* today, we will have a very successful party.
如果今天一切進展順利,我們將有一個成功的宴會。

go through 經歷;
檢查

Mr. Jones and his family had to *go through* a lot of hardship after he lost his job. 在瓊斯先生失業後,他和他的家人必須經歷許多苦難。

I have *gone through* all my desk drawers, but I still can't find my keys.
我已經檢查過書桌的所有抽屜,但還是找不到我的鑰匙。

go wrong 出錯;
有問題

I had a feeling something would *go wrong* with the software program, and now the computer has crashed.
我覺得這個軟體程式會有問題,所以現在電腦當機了。

guard against 防止；
使免於

Wash your hands frequently to *guard against* illness.
要常洗手，以免生病。

gunnery sergeant
槍砲軍士

A *gunnery sergeant* in the marines holds rank equivalent to that of a sergeant first class in the army.
海軍陸戰隊的槍砲軍士，和陸軍裡的上士，擁有同等的階級。

hand in 繳交

We were told to *hand in* our papers by Friday.
我們被告知，要在星期五前交報告。

Please *hand in* your weapon as soon as you finish target practice.
請一做完打靶練習，就將你的武器繳回。

hang around 閒蕩；
徘徊

I don't want to *hang around* and wait for the store to open; let's come back later.
我不想在附近閒蕩，等這家店開門；我們待會兒再回來。

hang on to 保留

Be sure to *hang on to* your receipt in case there is any problem with the product. 一定要保留你的收據，以防萬一產品有任何問題。

have got 有 | The Smiths *have got* three children, but one is away at school.
史密斯家有三個小孩，但有一個去上學了。

have got to 必須 | All visitors *have got to* register at the gate.
所有的訪客都必須在大門登記。

have in mind 打算；想要 | I'm looking for a new car. What I *have in mind* is a four-door that gets good gas mileage.
我正在找一輛新車。我想要的是有四門，而且每公升汽油里程數多的車。

have…over 邀請…（到家）作客 | The Nelsons have treated us to dinner twice. We should *have* them *over* for dinner soon. 尼爾森一家人，已經請我們吃過兩次晚餐了。我們應該在不久之後，請他們過來吃晚餐。

help *yourself* 自行取用 | *Help yourself* to some coffee; it's on the table over there.
自己去倒些咖啡吧；就在那裡的桌上。

if not 如果不是；如果沒有 | You had better finish your assignment on time. *If not*, you may not pass the course. 你最好準時完成作業。如果沒有的話，你這門課程可能無法及格。

in a rush 匆忙的　　It is easy to forget things when you are *in a rush*.

在你很匆忙的時候，容易忘記事情。

in a way 在某種程度上　　*In a way*, English is similar to German.

英語和德語，在某種程度上是相似的。

in accordance with 依照　　If you do not behave *in accordance with* the school rules, you may get into trouble.

如果你不依照校規行事，你可能會有麻煩。

in addition 此外　　I cleaned the house on Saturday. *In addition*, I mowed the lawn.

我星期六必須打掃房子。此外，我還除草。

in addition to 除了…之外　　We will visit Italy *in addition to* Germany and France.

我們除了去德國和法國之外，還會去義大利玩。

in all 共計　　There are 12 boys and 14 girls *in all* in my class.

我們班上總共有十二個男生，和十四個女生。

in case 以防萬一

Let's take a map *in case* we get lost.
我們帶張地圖，以防萬一迷路。

in case of 在…時候

The public should know what to do *in case of* an emergency.
民眾應該知道，緊急情況發生時，該怎麼辦。

in charge of 負責管理

The officer *in charge of* the investigation questioned the suspect.
那名負責調查的警官，審問那名嫌疑犯。

in common 共同的

The boys have many interests *in common*. For example, they both like swimming and tennis.
這兩個男孩有許多共同的興趣。例如，他們都喜歡游泳和網球。

in comparison with
和～相比

This book is quite easy to understand *in comparison with* the last one.
這本書和上一本比起來，相當容易了解。

in conclusion 總之

Dr. Stephens said, *in conclusion*, that he was sure he could prove his theory through further testing.
總之，史蒂芬斯博士說，他有把握可以透過更進一步的測試，來證明他的理論。

in connection with
與…有關

Now let's talk about fund-raising *in connection with* the new library.
現在,我們來討論有關新圖書館的募款活動。

in exchange for 交換

I gave Mary my blue pencil *in exchange for* her red one.
我給瑪麗藍色鉛筆,跟她交換紅色鉛筆。

The bank teller gave me three hundred and forty NT dollars *in exchange for* ten U.S. dollars. 銀行出納員用新台幣三百四十元,跟我換美金十元。

in full bloom 盛開

The garden looks beautiful now that all the flowers are *in full bloom*.
由於所有的花都盛開了,所以花園看起來很美。

in general 大致上;
一般而言

The children are very good *in general*, but sometimes they fight.
這些孩子大致上都很乖,但有時會打架。

In general, it rains a lot in summer, but this year it has not.
一般而言,夏天會下很多雨,但今年卻沒有。

in order 妥當的；
井然有序的

You will have no trouble getting a visa as long as your papers are *in order*.
只要你備妥文件，就能順利拿到簽證。

When the colonel inspects the barracks he will expect to find everything *in order*. 當上校視察營房時，他會期望看到每樣東西都井然有序。

in place of 代替

The vice-president attended the meeting *in place of* the president.
副總統代替總統出席這場會議。

in regard to 關於

In regard to your request for a refund, I'm afraid we cannot grant it unless you have the original receipt.
關於你要求退錢的事，恐怕我們無法同意，除非你有原來的收據。

in short 總之

I have to write an essay for English class, read two chapters in my history book, and finish my math assignment. *In short*, I have a lot of work to do.
我必須寫一篇英文課的論文，唸歷史課本兩章，還要完成我的數學作業。總之，我有很多作業要做。

in spite of 儘管

The sergeant ordered his men to complete the hike *in spite of* the rain. 儘管下著雨，中士還是命令他的士兵們，要完成健行。

in that case 那樣的話

Tina may not be able to come tomorrow. *In that case*, there will be only five people for lunch. 蒂娜明天可能沒辦法來。那樣的話，明天將只有五個人吃午餐。

in the course of 在⋯過程中

The chairman was interrupted several times by questions from the audience *in the course of* his speech. 在主席發表演說的過程中，被聽眾的問題打斷了好幾次。

in the event of 萬一

In the event of fire, exit the building immediately. 萬一發生火災，要立刻離開這棟建築物。

in the event that 如果

Use your cell phone to call me *in the event that* you get lost. 如果你迷路了，就用手機打電話給我。

in the face of 面臨；不管

The team was pessimistic about their chance of winning the game *in the face of* their opponent's greater skill and speed. 這支隊伍面臨對手較高超的技術和速度，所以對贏得比賽的可能性感到悲觀。

in the first place
首先;第一

I believe that I am the best person for the job. *In the first place*, I have a lot of experience, and second, I have a good relationship with all of our clients. 我相信我是做這份工作的最佳人選。首先,我的經驗豐富;第二,我和我們所有的客戶關係都很好。

in the meantime
在這段期間;同時

Dinner won't be ready for another hour. Let's have a drink *in the meantime*. 晚餐要再過一個小時才會好。我們在這段期間,先喝一杯吧。

I have to go to the post office. *In the meantime*, you can wash the dishes. 我必須去郵局。在這段期間,你可以洗碗盤。

in the same way
同樣地

The twins are so much alike that they even walk *in the same way*.
這對雙胞胎很相像,甚至連走路的樣子,都一模一樣。

in/on behalf of
為了…;代表…

The woman asked for a discount *on behalf of* her mother.
這位女士為她媽媽要求折扣。

Because Peter was ill, Joan spoke *in his behalf*. 因為彼得生病了,所以瓊恩代他發言。

just as 就像

I left my jacket in the restaurant, but when I went back I found it on the chair *just as* I had left it.

我把夾克留在餐廳裡，但當我回去找時，發現夾克就像我離開時一樣，還在椅子上。

just in time 正好及時

We got to the airport *just in time*. The plane was about to take off.

我們正好及時抵達機場。飛機即將要起飛了。

I went outside *just in time* to see the solar eclipse.

我走到外面時，正好來得及看見日蝕。

keep…away from
使…遠離

You must *keep* sharp objects *away from* the baby.

你必須使尖銳的物品遠離嬰兒。

keep track of
隨時注意

The old man *keeps track of* what is going on in the world by talking to his friends. 這個老人靠著和朋友交談，隨時注意世界上發生的事。

keep up with
趕上；跟上

Ted ran so fast that I could not *keep up with* him.

泰德跑得太快，以致於我無法趕上他。

key in 輸入

You have to *key in* your password if you want to use the computer.
如果你要使用這部電腦，就必須輸入你的密碼。

lack of 缺乏

The children are small for their age due to a *lack of* good nutrition.
由於缺乏良好的營養，這些孩子就他們的年齡來說，太矮小了。

lance corporal 上等兵

My cousin is a *lance corporal* in the marine corps.
我堂弟是海軍陸戰隊的上等兵。

learn a lesson 得到教訓

I *learned a* valuable *lesson* when I was stopped by the police for speeding.
當我因超速行駛而被警方攔下來時，我得到了珍貴的教訓。

leave out 遺漏

The cake did not taste good because I accidentally *left out* one of the ingredients. 這個蛋糕不好吃，因為我無意中遺漏了其中一種原料。

lend a hand 幫助

The work will be easy to finish if everyone *lends a hand*.
如果每個人都來幫忙，這個工作很容易就能完成。

lie down 躺下來

The doctor asked the patient to *lie down* on the examination table.
醫生要求這名病人躺在檢查台上。

lieutenant commnader 少校

Kim is a *lieutenant commander* in the navy.
金姆是一位海軍少校。

lieutenant general 中將

A *lieutenant general* wears three stars on his uniform.
中將的制服上有三顆星。

lieutenant junior grade 中尉

The *lieutenant junior grade* hopes to be promoted to lieutenant this year.
這名中尉希望今年可以升上尉。

light bulb 燈泡

The lamp doesn't work because the *light bulb* has burned out.
因為燈泡燒壞了，所以這盞燈不會亮。

line up 排隊；排列

You must *line up* and wait for service at the post office.
在郵局，你必須排隊等候服務。

The teacher asked me to *line up* the books on the shelf.
老師要求我，將這些書排在架子上。

little by little 一點
一點地；漸漸地

I am saving for a new car *little by little*. By next spring I should be able to afford one.

我為了買新車而一點一點地儲蓄。到了明年春天，我應該就買得起了。

live on 以…維生

Ian turned down the job because the salary was too low to *live on*.

伊恩拒絕了這份工作，因為薪水太低，無法維生。

live wire 通電的電線

If you touch a *live wire*, you may get a shock.

如果你去碰通電的電線，你可能會觸電。

look after 照顧

Could you *look after* my dog while I am on vacation? 在我去渡假的時候，你可不可以照顧我的狗？

look down on
瞧不起；往下看

The boy *looked down on* his classmate just because he came from a poor family. 這個男孩看不起他同學，只因為他同學是來自貧困的家庭。

look forward to
期待

The recruits are really *looking forward to* their first leave.

這些新兵非常期待第一次的休假。

look in on 順道探望

The nurse decided to *look in on* the paitent and make sure that he was all right. 這名護士決定順道探望一下那名病患，以確定他安然無恙。

look into 調查

The journalist discovered the official's crime when he *looked into* his past.
當記者調查這名官員的來歷時，發現了他所犯的罪。

look up to 尊敬；崇拜

Teenagers often *look up to* sports stars and want to be just like them.
十幾歲的青少年常會崇拜運動明星，而且想要和他們一樣。

lose *one's* **temper**
發脾氣

I am afraid my father will *lose his temper* when he hears about my bad grades. 我怕當我爸爸聽到我的爛成績時，會發脾氣。

lose track of 忘記

The parade was so much fun to watch that I *lost track of* time.
看遊行很有趣，使我忘了時間。

major general 少將

A *major general* is a two-star general.
少將是二星級的將官。

make sense 合理

Saying that two plus two is five does not *make sense*.

說二加二等於五,是不合理的。

make sure 確定

Please *make sure* that the dog has enough water before you go out.

在你出門前,請確定小狗有足夠的水。

make up 編造;和好

When Tom is late for school he *makes up* an excuse.

當湯姆上學遲到時,他編造了一個藉口。

After their argument, the two friends did not speak to one another for a while, but eventually they *made up*.

在爭辯過後,這兩個朋友暫時不跟對方說話,但最後還是和好了。

Marine Corps
海軍陸戰隊

The *Marine Corps* is one of the four branches of military service.

海軍陸戰隊是兵役的四個分支之一。

master chief petty officer 一級軍士長

A *master chief petty officer* outranks a senior chief petty officer.

一級軍士長的階級,比二級軍士長高。

master sergeant
士官長

A *master sergeant* in the army is equivalent in rank to a master sergeant in the marines.
陸軍士官長的階級，和海軍陸戰隊士官長的階級，是相等的。

mess up 搞砸；做錯

The boy's poor score on the math final *messed up* his chances of getting the scholarship. 這個男孩在數學期末考的成績很差，搞砸了得獎學金的機會。

I am going to practice the drill. If you see me *mess up*, please tell me what I did wrong.
我將按正確的步驟練習。如果你看到我做錯，請告訴我哪邊錯了。

neglect to 疏忽；忘記

The thief was able to get in because I *neglected to* lock the door.
因為我忘記鎖門，小偷才會跑進來。

no matter who/ what/where
無論是誰 / 什麼 / 何處

You must obey the law *no matter who* you are.
無論你是誰，都必須守法。

no place 到處都沒有

There is *no place* to park on this street. Let's try the next one. 這條街上到處都沒有地方停車。我們試試下一條街吧。

noncommissioned officer 士官
（簡稱 *NCO*）

If you want to become a *noncommissioned officer*, you must show that you have leadership skills.
如果你要成為一名士官，你必須顯露出你的領導能力。

object to 反對；抗議

The customer *objected to* the clerk's rude behavior.
這名顧客抗議店員無禮的態度。

on account of 因為

The student fainted *on account of* the heat.
這名學生因為太熱而昏倒了。

on and on 不停地

Although the audience was bored, the speaker went *on and on*.
儘管聽眾們都感到厭煩了，演講者還是不停地說著。

on top of 在…的上面

Just put those papers *on top of* the pile; I'll look at them later.
就把那些報告放在這堆上面；我待會會看。

once again 再一次

Please do the dance step *once again* so that I can see how you do it.
請再示範一次舞步，以便讓我看清楚你是怎麼跳的。

once and for all
永遠地

We have had the TV repaired many times. Let's just buy a new one and solve the problem *once and for all*.
這台電視已經修理了很多次了。我們就買一台新的，永遠解決這個問題吧。

once in a while
偶爾

Patty usually swims in the school swimming pool, but *once in a while* she goes to the beach.
派蒂通常都在學校的游泳池游泳，但有時也會到海邊去。

once more 再一次

Let's ride the roller coaster *once more* before we go home.
在回家之前，我們再去坐一次雲霄飛車吧。

one after another
一個接一個地

He ate the cookies *one after another* until they were all gone.
他一片接一片地吃著餅乾，直到全部吃完為止。

one another 互相

We usually give *one another* presents on Christmas.
我們通常會在聖誕節時互相送禮物。

pass away 去世

My grandmother was 90 years old when she *passed away*.
我祖母過世時已經九十歲了。

pass on 傳遞

When I finish this magazine I will *pass* it *on* to my brother.
當我看完這本雜誌時，我會傳給我弟弟。

pass out 昏倒

The medical student *passed out* the first time he saw blood.
這名醫學系學生，在第一次看到血時昏倒了。

pay attention to 注意

It is important to *pay attention to* safety instructions because they could save your life. 注意安全指示是很重要的，因為它們可能會救你一命。

petty officer （海軍）士官（= *sergeant*）

There are three classes of *petty officer* in the navy.
海軍裡有三種階級的士官。

physical training 體能訓練

All of the new recruits must complete the *physical training*.
所有的新兵都必須完成體能訓練。

pick up 學會

After one month in Japan, I had *picked up* enough Japanese to have a simple conversation.
在日本一個月之後，我就學會了足夠應付簡單對話的日語。

potato salad 馬鈴薯沙拉

The ***potato salad*** served at the picnic was delicious.

野餐時供應的馬鈴薯沙拉很好吃。

prior to 在⋯之前

You must pay the tuition ***prior to*** the first day of class.

你必須在第一天上課之前,繳清學費。

private first class 上等兵

When the soldier was promoted from private to ***private first class***, he received an insignia for his uniform.

當這名士兵由二等兵升為一等兵時,他得到一枚別在制服上的勳章。

pull apart 拆開

The pages of the newspaper were stuck together and they tore when I tried to ***pull*** them ***apart***.

報紙的幾個版面黏在一起了,當我試著拆開時,卻把它們撕破了。

pull through 脫離險境

The driver was seriously injured in the accident, but it looks like he will ***pull through***.

這名駕駛人在車禍中受重傷,但看起來他將會脫離險境。

put across
傳達…（給某人）

William was able to *put* the proposal *across* so well that the committee approved it unanimously.

威廉將計劃表達得很好，所以全體的委員都一致同意。

put aside 儲存

I *put aside* some money every month because I am saving for a new car.

我每個月會存一些錢，因為我要存錢買新車。

put away 收拾；整理

Please *put* all the art materials *away* when you have finished working.

當你完成工作後，請將所有的美術材料收拾好。

put together 拼湊；組合

This puzzle is too difficult for the children to *put together*.

這個拼圖對小孩來說，太難拼了。

put up with 忍受

I have to *put up with* a lot of noise because I live near the airport.

因為我住在機場附近，所以必須忍受許多噪音。

quiet down
安靜下來；平息；減少

Please *quiet down* so that Mr. Allen can announce the election results.

請安靜下來，好讓艾倫先生宣佈選舉結果。

quite a few 相當多的

When the test was over, there were still *quite a few* questions I hadn't answered; I doubt I passed.
當考試時間結束時，我還有相當多問題沒有回答；我懷疑我是否能及格。

rain check （受邀的一方一時不能應邀時）請對方下次再邀的要求

I'd love to go to a movie with you, but I'm busy tonight. How about a *rain check*? 我很想和你一起去看電影，但我今晚沒空。下次再一起去看如何？

rather than 而不是

The test was an oral one *rather than* a written exam.
這次的考試是口試，而不是筆試。

real estate 不動產；房地產

Sarah wants to buy some *real estate* as an investment, so she is looking at houses today. 莎拉想買一些房地產作為投資，所以她今天去看房子了。

rear admiral 海軍少將

The rank of *rear admiral* in the navy is equivalent to that of a major general in the army.
海軍少將的階級，和陸軍少將是同等的。

regardless of 不管

We must have the roof fixed *regardless of* how much it costs.
不管花多少錢，我們都得將屋頂修好。

relating to
與…有關；關於

There is nothing in today's paper *relating to* the bank robbery yesterday.
今天的報紙，沒有昨天的銀行搶案的相關報導。

rely on 依賴

I know I can *rely on* you to keep our plans a secret. 我知道我可以信賴你，會將我們的計畫保密。

result from 起因於

The collapse of the building *resulted from* the poor construction.
這棟建築物會倒塌，是由於結構不佳。

result in 導致；造成

Cheating on the test will *result in* expulsion from school.
考試作弊會造成被學校開除的結果。

rock music 搖滾樂

Lisa likes classical music, but she doesn't like the *rock music* her children listen to.
麗莎喜歡古典音樂，而不喜歡她的孩子聽的搖滾樂。

run across 偶然發現；碰巧遇到

If you *run across* my glasses while you are cleaning up, please tell me.
當你在打掃時，如果偶然發現我的眼鏡，請告訴我。

run short of 不夠；
短缺

You have invited so many people to the party that if everyone attends, we will *run short of* food.

你邀請太多人來參加宴會了，所以如果每個人都到，我們的食物會不夠。

sea level 海平面；海拔

The mountain peak is nearly 3000 meters above *sea level*.

這座山的山頂，將近海拔三千公尺。

seaman apprentice
（美國海軍或海岸警衛隊中的）三等兵

The insignia of a *seaman apprentice* has two stripes.

三等兵的徽章上有兩道條紋。

seaman recruit
（美國海軍或海岸警衛隊中低於三等兵的）新水兵

A *seaman recruit* holds the lowest rank in the navy.

新水兵的階級，是海軍當中最低的。

see about 安排；處理

We visited the restaurant to *see about* holding a private party there.

我們參觀了那家餐廳，以安排在那邊舉辦私人宴會的事。

senior chief petty officer （美國海軍或海岸警衛隊）二級軍士長

A *senior chief petty officer* holds the rank of E-8 in the navy.

二級軍士長在海軍的階級是第八級。

senior master sergeant （美國空軍）
二級士官長

The rank of *senior master sergeant* is found only in the air force.
二級士官長這個階級，只有美國空軍才有。

sergeant first class
（美國陸軍）上士

The rank of *sergeant first class* in the army is equivalent to that of master sergeant in the air force.
陸軍上士的階級，相當於空軍士官長。

sergeant major 士官長
（美國陸軍、空軍和海軍陸戰隊各級司令部，尤指團級司令部中，指揮官的行政助理）

The rank of *sergeant major* is found in both the army and the marine corps.
士官長這個階級，在陸軍和海軍陸戰隊裡都有。

set off 啓動；出發

The burglar *set off* the alarm when he opened the window.
這名夜賊在打開窗戶時，啓動了警報器。

set out 出發；陳列

We must *set out* at 6:00 tomorrow morning if we want to arrive by noon.
如果我們想中午以前抵達，就必須在明天早上六點出發。

shut down 關閉

Remember to *shut down* the computer before you leave.

在你離開之前，記得將電腦關掉。

sick call （軍隊中）病號集合就診時間

The clinic holds *sick call* from 9:00 to 11:00, but if it is an emergency, you can go directly to the hospital.

這間診所的就診時間從九點到十一點，但若是緊急情況，你可以直接到醫院去。

sign in/out 簽到（退）

All visitors are required to *sign in* at the gate and to *sign out* again when they leave.

所有的訪客被要求在大門口簽到，而且當他們離去時，還要再簽退。

since then 從那時起

I went to Kenting two years ago, but I haven't been back *since then*.

我兩年前去了墾丁，而從那時起，我就再也沒有回去過。

soak up 吸入；吸收

The janitor used a towel to *soak up* the water that had come in through the open window.

大樓管理員用一條毛巾，來吸從打開的窗戶所滲入的水。

social security card
社會安全卡

The company asks that all new employees show their *social security cards* as proof that they can work legally in the United States.

這家公司要求所有的新進員工，出示他們的社會安全卡，以作爲他們能合法地在美國工作的證明。

social security number 社會安全號碼

Your *social security number* is required on many official documents.

你的社會安全號碼，在許多正式的文件上都會用得到。

staff sergeant
（美國）參謀軍士

Owen was promoted from sergeant to *staff sergeant*.

歐文從中士被升爲參謀軍士。

stand by 站在旁邊；
支持

I know my family will *stand by* me no matter what happens.

我知道無論發生什麼事，我的家人都會支持我。

stand for 代表；容忍；
允許

What does the initial in your name *stand for*?

你名字的起首字母是代表什麼？

The teacher is very strict and will not *stand for* lateness.

這位老師非常嚴厲，不允許遲到。

start out (on) 開始

Mary will *start out on* her trip around the world next week.

瑪麗將在下星期，開始她環遊世界的旅程。

stay away from 遠離

The principal warned the students to *stay away from* drugs.

校長警告學生們，要遠離毒品。

stay over 在外住宿

We had such a good time at the beach that we decided to *stay over* for a few more days. 我們在海邊玩得很愉快，所以我們決定要多住幾天。

stay up 熬夜

We all *stayed up* late to watch the World Cup Final.

我們大家都因為看世界盃決賽，而熬夜到很晚。

stick out 突出；伸出；顯眼

Mr. Brown's house really *sticks out*; it's the only purple one on the street.

布朗先生的房子非常顯眼；它是街上唯一的一棟紫色的房子。

stick to 堅持；持之以恆地做

If you *stick to* your diet for another month, you will lose another five kilos. 如果你再持續節食一個月，你就可以再減五公斤。

swimming pool
游泳池

Do you prefer to go to the *swimming pool* or to the beach?
你比較喜歡去游泳池還是海邊？

switch off 關掉（開關）

Don't forget to *switch off* the light when you go out.
當你出門時，別忘了關燈。

switch on 打開（開關）

It's hot in here; let's *switch on* the fan.
這裡很熱；我們把電風扇打開吧。

take a chance 碰運氣

We decided to *take a chance* and bought some lottery tickets.
我們決定碰碰運氣，買了幾張彩券。

take action 採取行動

After the accident, Linda was the first to *take action* and call the police.
車禍發生後，琳達是第一個採取行動，通知警方的人。

take advantage of
利用

Ted decided to *take advantage of* his uncle's offer to pay for his college education. 泰德決定利用他叔叔主動提供的金錢，來支付他的大學教育費用。

take after 相像

The boy *takes after* his father in every way.
這個男孩從各方面看，都像他父親。

take apart 分解;拆開

I will have to *take* the air conditioner *apart* to find out what is wrong with it. 我必須將冷氣機拆開,才能找出哪邊發生故障。

take care of 照顧

He asked me to *take care of* his dog while he was away. 他要求我在他不在時,照顧他的狗。

take charge (of) 擔任;負責

If anything happens to the president, the vice-president must be ready to *take charge*. 如果總統發生了任何事,副總統必須準備好接任。

William will agree to *take charge of* the project if we relieve him of his duties. 如果我們減輕威廉的責任,他就會答應負責這項計畫。

take effect 生效

The new parking restrictions will *take effect* next month. 新的停車限制,將在下個月生效。

take inventory 清查存貨;存貨盤查

The library is closed today so that the staff can *take inventory*. 圖書館今天休館,以便工作人員清查圖書。

take it out on
找…出氣

Whenever Billy has trouble at school, he *takes it out on* his little sister.
每當比利在學校遇到困難時,他都會把氣出在他的小妹身上。

take leave 離開;告別

I usually *take leave* in February because I like to ski. 我通常在二月份時離開,因為我喜歡去滑雪。

take off 出發;休假;脫掉;起飛

We had better *take off* now if we want to get home on time.
如果我們想準時到家,最好現在就出發。

George will *take* next Friday *off* because he has to go to the dentist.
喬治下週五要休假,因為他必須去看牙醫。

take on 承擔;雇用

Ted will *take on* more of the housework when his wife goes back to work.
當泰德的妻子回去上班後,他將要負擔更多的家事。

take part in 參加

All of the students will be required to *take part in* the school athletic program.
所有的學生都將被要求參加學校的體育課程。

take turns 輪流

We have only one car so we *take turns* using it.
我們只有一部車，所以我們輪流開。

take up 從事（工作、興趣等）

The doctor suggested that I *take up* jogging in order to lose weight.
醫生建議我，利用慢跑來減重。

talk back to 跟…頂嘴

Don't *talk back to* the teacher or you will get in trouble.
不要跟老師頂嘴，否則你會惹上麻煩。

technical sergeant
（美國空軍）技術士官

The rank of *technical sergeant* is found only in the air force.
技術士官這個階級，只有空軍才有。

think up 想出

He was punished when he could not *think up* a good excuse for being late.
他因為想不出遲到的好藉口，所以被處罰了。

try out 試試；試用

We decided to *try out* the new restaurant that everyone is talking about.
我們決定要去試試大家都在談論的那家新餐廳。

turn down 關小聲

Please *turn down* the radio; I'm on the phone.

請將收音機關小聲；我正在講電話。

turn over 移交；
將…翻過來

When you go on vacation, *turn over* your work to one of your colleagues.

當你去渡假時，要將你的工作移交給同事。

After filling one side of the paper, she *turned* it *over* and continued to write on the back. 在這張紙的一面寫滿後，她將紙翻過來，繼續在背面寫。

turn up 開大聲

Would you *turn up* the television, please? I can barely hear it.

可以請你將電視開大聲一點嗎？我幾乎聽不到。

use up 用完

Making this cake will *use up* all the flour; we should buy some more.

做這個蛋糕會用掉所有的麵粉；我們應該再買一些。

vice admiral 中將

A *vice admiral* reports to an admiral.

中將要向上將報到。

want ad 徵人廣告；
徵求廣告

The couple looked through the *want ads*, hoping to find an inexpensive apartment.

這對夫婦看遍了徵求廣告，希望能找到便宜的公寓。

warrant officer
（美國海軍）士官長

A *warrant officer* has a rank of W-1.

美國海軍士官長的官階是 W-1。

work out 解決

This is a difficult situation, but I know we can find a way to *work it out*.

這是個麻煩的情況，但是我知道，我們可以找出解決的方法。

would rather 寧願

Jim wants to see a comedy, but I *would rather* see a horror movie.

吉姆想看喜劇，但我寧願看恐怖片。

zip code 郵遞區號

Remember to write the *zip code* on the envelope if you want the letter to arrive without delay.

如果你想要信件立刻送達，記得在信封上寫郵遞區號。

ECL 新試題得分關鍵字

admissible 〔 əd'mɪsəb̜ḷ 〕 adj. 可接受的

aerospace 〔'ɛrəˏspes 〕 n. 大氣層及太空；航太

ailment 〔'elmənt 〕 n. 疾病

augur 〔'ɔgɚ 〕 v. 預言；顯示

aurora 〔 ɔ'rɔrə 〕 n. (南、北極的) 極光

barrack 〔'bærək 〕 n. 兵營

bomber 〔'bamɚ 〕 n. 轟炸機

BOQ 單身軍官宿舍 (= *bachelor officers' quarters*)

BX 空軍基地的免稅百貨商店
(= *Base Exchange*)
陸軍的是 PX (= *Post Exchange*)
海軍的是 NEX (= *Naval Exchange*)

callous 〔'kæləs 〕 adj. 無情的

cartographer 〔 kar'tagrəfɚ 〕 n. 製圖者

casualties 〔'kæʒuəltɪz 〕 n. pl. 傷亡人員

chalk 〔 tʃɔk 〕 n. 粉筆

chapel 〔'tʃæpḷ 〕 n. 小教堂

chestnut 〔'tʃɛsnət 〕 adj. 褐色的

chunk 〔 tʃʌŋk 〕 n. 許多

cleaners 〔'klinɚz 〕 n. 洗衣店

combustion 〔 kəm'bʌstʃən 〕 n. 燃燒

commissary 〔'kaməˏsɛrɪ 〕 n. 軍中超級市場

compile 〔 kəm'paɪl 〕 v. 編輯

conceited 〔 kən'sitɪd 〕 adj. 自負的

dampness 〔'dæmpnɪs 〕 n. 濕氣

dashboard 〔'dæʃˏbord 〕 n. 儀表板

dazzle 〔'dæzḷ 〕 v. 使目眩；使驚訝

dehydrated 〔 di'haɪdretɪd 〕 adj. 脫水的

depot 〔'dipo 〕 n. 倉庫

deteriorate 〔 dɪ'tɪrɪəˏret 〕 v. 惡化

dictate 〔'dɪktet 〕 v. 聽寫

discolored 〔 dɪs'kʌlɚd 〕 adj. 變色的

dished 〔 dɪʃt 〕 adj. 凹下的

disrupt 〔 dɪs'rʌpt 〕 v. 使破裂

dissipate 〔'dɪsəˏpet 〕 v. 驅散

drizzle 〔'drɪzḷ 〕 n. 毛毛雨

echelon 〔'ɛʃəˏlan 〕 n. 指揮階級

emblem 〔'ɛmbləm 〕 n. 象徵；標幟

enlisted man 士兵

exorbitant 〔 ɪg'zɔrbətənt 〕 adj. 過分的

extemporaneously 〔 本字在 ECL 中考拼字〕
〔 ɪkˏstɛmpə'renɪəslɪ 〕 adv. 即席地

falsify 〔'fɔlsəˏfaɪ 〕 v. 偽造

fan 〔 fæn 〕 n. 風扇

finicky 〔'fɪnɪkɪ 〕 adj. 苛求的

forfeit 〔'fɔrfɪt 〕 v. 喪失

freight 〔 fret 〕 n. 貨物

fuse 〔 fjuz 〕 n. (炸彈的) 導火線；引信

gear 〔 gɪr 〕 n. 齒輪

gem 〔 dʒɛm 〕 n. 寶石

generic 〔 dʒə'nɛrɪk 〕 adj. 一般的

gravel 〔'grævḷ 〕 n. 碎石子

gunnery 〔'gʌnərɪ 〕 n. 槍砲

haul 〔 hɔl 〕 v. 運輸；拖

hit the sack 上床睡覺

honoree 〔ˏanə'ri 〕 n. 受獎者

immaterial 〔ˏɪmə'tɪrɪəl 〕 adj. 不重要的

immerse 〔 ɪ'mɝs 〕 v. 使專注於

inoculate 〔 ɪn'akjəˏlet 〕 v. 接種 (疫苗)

insecticide 〔 ɪn'sɛktəˏsaɪd 〕 n. 殺蟲劑

intensely 〔 ɪn'tɛnslɪ 〕 adv. 緊張地

jet-propulsion (ˈdʒɛtprəˈpʌlʃən)
adj. 噴射推進的

jot (dʒat) *n.* 些微；少量

kerosene (ˈkɛrəˌsin) *n.* 煤油

knob (nab) *n.* 圓形把手

knowingly (ˈnoɪŋlɪ) *adv.* 故意地

latent (ˈletn̩t) *adj.* 潛在的

linear (ˈlɪnɪɚ) *adj.* 直線的

linkage (ˈlɪŋkɪdʒ) 連鎖；磁鏈

logistics (loˈdʒɪstɪks) *n.* 後方勤務；
後勤學

lubricant (ˈlubrɪkənt) *n.* 潤滑油

lubrication (ˌlubrɪˈkeʃən) *n.*
潤滑；上油

lumber (ˈlʌmbɚ) *n.* 木材

muddy (ˈmʌdɪ) *adj.* 混濁的

NCO 士官 (= *noncommissioned*
officer)

nickel (ˈnɪkl̩) *n.* 五分錢硬幣

occlude (əˈklud) *v.* 封閉；(牙齒
的) 咬合

partible(ˈpartəbl̩) *adj.* 可分的

partition (parˈtɪʃən) *n.* 隔板

pasteboard (ˈpestˌbord) *n.* 紙板

pastry (ˈpestrɪ) *n.* 酥皮糕餅

perforate (ˈpɝfəˌret) *v.* 穿孔

peripheral (pəˈrɪfərəl) *adj.* 外圍的

piston (ˈpɪstn̩) *n.* 活塞

poise (pɔɪz) *n.* 平衡；平靜

porous (ˈporəs) *adj.* 多孔的

pottery (ˈpatɚɪ) *n.* 陶器

preliminary (prɪˈlɪməˌnɛrɪ) *adj.*
初步的

prognosticate (pragˈnastɪˌket)
v. 預測

propulsion (prəˈpʌlʃən) *n.* 推進力

pungent (ˈpʌndʒənt) *adj.* 嚴厲的

ranger (ˈrendʒɚ) *n.* 森林管理員

rainfall (ˈrenˌfɔl) *n.* 降雨

rearview mirror 後照鏡

recurrent (rɪˈkɝənt) *adj.* 反覆
出現的

reel (ril) *n.* (釣竿上的) 線軸

reinforce (ˌriɪnˈfors) *v.* 加強

rib (rɪb) *n.* 肋骨

rink (rɪŋk) *n.* 溜冰場

scarf (skarf) *n.* 圍巾

sheetrock (ˈʃitˈrak) *n.* 石膏板

shipment (ˈʃɪpmənt) *n.* 裝載的貨物

sleet (slit) *v.* 下雨雪

sponge (spʌndʒ) *n.* 海綿

stab (stæb) *v.* 刺傷

stall (stɔl) *v.* 使停止　　*n.* 攤位

static (ˈstætɪk) *adj.* 靜止的

stub (stʌb) *n.* (票的) 存根

sulfur (ˈsʌlfɚ) *n.* 硫；硫磺

supposedly (səˈpozɪdlɪ) *adv.* 根據
推測

tarnished (ˈtarnɪʃt) *adj.* 變色的

thermonuclear (ˌθɝmoˈnjuklɪɚ)
adj. 熱核反應的

thermostat (ˈθɝməˌstæt) *n.* 自動
調溫器

torch (tɔrtʃ) *n.* 火把；手電筒

tract (trækt) *n.* 區域

tractor (ˈtræktɚ) *n.* 拖曳機

undercover (ˌʌndɚˈkʌvɚ) *adj.*
暗中進行的

underfed (ˌʌndɚˈfɛd) *adj.* 營養
不良的

vertically (ˈvɝtɪklɪ) *adv.* 垂直地

whirl (hwɝl) *n.* 旋轉

whooping crane (ˈhwupɪŋˈkren)
n. 美洲鶴

woodland (ˈwʊdˌlænd) *n.* 林地

ECL 字彙
ECL Vocabulary

售價：380 元

主　　編／劉　毅

發　行　所／學習出版有限公司　　　☎ (02) 2704-5525

郵撥帳號／05127272 學習出版社帳戶

登　記　證／局版台業 2179 號

印　刷　所／裕強彩色印刷有限公司

台北門市／台北市許昌街 17 號 6F　　☎ (02) 2331-4060

台灣總經銷／紅螞蟻圖書有限公司　　☎ (02) 2795-3656

本公司網址／www.learnbook.com.tw

電子郵件／learnbook@learnbook.com.tw

2021 年 1 月 1 日新修訂

4713269384083